MOSHPIT

The Violent World of Mosh Pit Culture

Joe Ambrose

OMNIBUS PRESS
LONDON · NEW YORK · SYDNEY

Cover designed by Phil Gambrill
Picture research by Nikki Lloyd

ISBN: 0.7119.8744.0
UK Order No: OP 48345
USA Order No: OP 48576

Exclusive Distributors:
Music Sales Limited,
8/9 Frith Street,
London W1D 3JB, UK.

Music Sales Corporation,
257 Park Avenue South,
New York, NY 10010, USA.

Macmillan Distribution Services,
53 Park West Drive,
Derrimut, Vic 3030,
Australia.

To the Music Trade only:
Music Sales Limited,
8/9 Frith Street,
London W1D 3JB, UK.

Every effort has been made to trace the copyright holders of the photographs in this book but one or two were unreachable. We would be grateful if the photographers concerned would contact us.

Typeset by Galleon Typesetting, Ipswich.
Printed in Great Britain by MPG Books Ltd, Bodmin, Cornwall.

A catalogue record for this book is available from the British Library.

www.omnibuspress.com

Contents

Moshing – An Introduction

Moshing is a ritualised and furious form of dancing combining very real violence with remarkable displays of emotion, life-and-death situations, and the raw sex beat of rock'n'roll. It induces euphoric displays of affection and hostility between its usually male participants.

It derives from the mid-Seventies punk practices of stage diving and slam dancing wherein spread-out gangs of punk kids at gigs would indulge in dancing, pogoing, and slamming into one another. The punks were giving expression to their profound lack of connection to the Old Guy Seventies music of Eric Clapton, The Eagles, etc. At Old Guy gigs the ageing collegiate types the punks so despised stood still in front of their heroes, clapping appreciatively, whistling, swaying, or sometimes cosmic dancing like they were attending some eternal Woodstock of the imagination.

In the late Seventies the punks were saying through their slam dancing that they were different, on the fringe, offensive. They were declaring themselves to be as alienated by traditional rock'n'roll values as they were by normal society. Gobbing, spitting at one another, at bands, at perceived enemies, was part of their strong *Stay Away* message. The punks were saying to the world that they were young and confident in their vision. They saw slam dancing as a new punk version of sex and violence. Like generations that went before

1

them, and others that followed, they were convinced that there was a connection between themselves, their music, and their community.

Long after the founding fathers of punk had retired to their mansions, websites, and fortunes, new waves on underground music exploded all over clandestine America. Reports came in that seething masses of youth were to be seen crashing into one another in front of small club stages. By the early Nineties these reports talked of brutal gut-wrenching violence, especially in New York hardcore clubs. The music being played by the bands was no longer the main thing happening in American rock clubs. People came to see the rage and fury, not to hear the music – which was also frenzied and furious.

Tightly packed crowds were seen to support others amongst themselves who were body surfing over their heads. The crowds did this by uplifting their own arms and holding surfers aloft. Another trick this new crowd had was stage diving, which usually consisted of either a member of the audience or a member of a band leaping from the stage into what came to be known as the mosh pit – the area in front of the stage where all this frenzied activity took place. This was the pastime, in the main, of stripped-to-the waist adolescent boys.

Sometimes, and it was always a feat worth seeing, stage diving involved the process in reverse. Brave members of the audience attempting to leap from the auditorium onto the stage or at least into the security pit which separates crowd from band, an area full of security guards (bouncers), and, sometimes, press photographers. Artists like Courtney Love from Hole became associated with stage diving into the mosh pit – it was her style when gigging with Hole to goad the pit into a pent-up state before diving in amongst her followers. It became the norm that she emerged from the pit half-naked.

Moshing is a combination of three main factors. Crowd

surfing, stage diving, and the slam dancing of the original punks taken to a new level of violence. It usually takes place in a semicircular space right in front of the stage, the heaviest and most violent moshing happening in front of the lead singer, but a little back from the security barriers. There are certain acts like Limp Bizkit, Kid Rock, and Slipknot, where the mosh pit extends to the entire auditorium or field where they are playing.

Sometimes there are circle pits, extraordinary expressions of solidarity in front of hardcore bands. A circle pit involves a large number of people – it needs a decent crowd – forming and running around in a huge circle, holding on to one another to maintain balance. The circle turns faster and faster as the music picks up speed. Circle pits are uniquely good humoured, a source of tender youthful joy to the participants, and are often instigated by bands when they see things getting a little tight or sour in the pit.

To the outsider moshing looks like the most terrifying spectacle, as if things have got totally out of control, as if hundreds will surely get badly injured. In fact there is a highly structured sense of community within a good pit. Sometimes there are kids there who are natural leaders and organisers. Often these are feral little guys concerned about the safety of those around them. Then again, sometimes there are pit lieutenants who've been sent in there by responsible bands who are concerned about things going wrong. These pit lieutenants are rarely bouncers or roadies, they're usually the given band's original camp followers – those who followed them from the earliest days – who now enjoy the confidence of both band and pit. Pearl Jam and the London band One Minute Silence have been particularly diligent in this regard.

In addition to these unobserved leaders there is also the concept of Pit Etiquette which is a common law shared by those who take the pit seriously. The fundamental rules of this

Etiquette insist that people look out for one another and react instantly when they see something going wrong. Sexual harassment of boys and girls is frowned upon, as is irresponsible crowd surfing and bullying. The idea of this Etiquette is that people should intervene communally when they see something they don't like. Violence is not forbidden by this Etiquette, as actual consensual violence is part of the dancing which happens in the pit.

What began in small clubs now stuffs arenas. The violence of the mosh pits, which ten years ago resulted in self-elected injuries shared between grown men, has spread out all over the place. Now the moshing is often carried out by as many as 50,000 people at one time. Many of the moshers are young teenage boys, many more are out-of-their-depth college girls, and an awful lot of moshers are huge muscle-bound jocks looking for a legal way to kick the shit out of one another or thinking with their cocks. There have been a few deaths in the pit. Many others have ended up paraplegic or with serious injuries. Minor injuries like broken arms and legs are the norm at any outdoor festival where the flag of rock'n'roll is raised. Broken noses and sprained ankles are no longer deemed serious. A free clinic in San Francisco's Haight Ashbury set up a Rock Medicine program devoted entirely to dealing with mosh injuries.

In 1994 two deaths attributed to mosh-related head injuries brought the issue into sharp focus. A 21-year-old guy died at a Motorhead gig in London while a 17-year-old died at a rock club in New York. That same year two moshing participants were made paraplegic at a Rhode Island Lollapalooza show and at a Sepultura/Pantera show in Maryland. Concert and club venues now live in terror of legal actions inspired by pit injuries and have taken to videotaping mosh pits in an effort to document the fact that moshers are bringing the danger upon themselves.

This is an attitude with which most moshers have some sympathy. "If you don't want to get injured, don't go into the pit," is the consistent message you get from pit veterans. This simple advice is exactly right. People know that they stand a chance of being injured or molested in the pit. The very presence of these dark dangers is what drives them in there and, conversely, gives them a comforting sense of belonging. In this sometimes hostile landscape, they have to look out for one another. There is more fraternity and harmony in the pit than outsiders can possibly imagine.

Moshing happens amongst several different tribes. Some of these tribes cross over into one another, as is only to be expected because most people like a few different styles of music.

Rapcore is a mixture of white rap and hardcore. The Red Hot Chili Peppers are the best band in that genre, while Limp Bizkit are the most popular. Nu-metal is essentially a pop version of rapcore, and leading exponents include the superlite Linkin Park and the humorous Bloodhound Gang. Skacore is often just punk with a brass section, like Less Than Jake.

Emocore, emotionally charged punk, is guitar-based mid-tempo rock played by bands like Fugazi. Originally bands on this scene did long drawn out songs with a vocal contrast between conventional singing, soft whispering, gut-wrenching screams, and actual crying or sobbing.

Grindcore sounds exactly like what the name implies, a grungy guitar noise assault founded by Napalm Death, and popularised by Biohazard and Suicidal Tendencies. It is a close relation of Death Metal, with which it shares an impressive brutality, downtuned guitars, and growled vocals. Whereas

Death Metal tunes can go on forever, Grindcore benefits from an economic punk brevity in songs which have either social conscience or angst-ridden lyrics.

Punk rock divides into hardcore punk, the outstandingly powerful scene from which moshing first emerged, and pop punk, an idiotic licence to print money. Pop punk superstars like Green Day and The Offspring play stadiums all over the world. Pop punk bears scant resemblance to punk but has strong roots in the lighter end of the New Wave which conquered America in the aftermath of Seventies punk.

And then there are about fifty other semi-obscure sub-genres in front of which people dance, riot, and inflict damage on one another.

As in all areas of art, in rock music the hardcore cutting edge, the real extreme stuff, has been used as a battering ram with which to sell the softer stuff. For every interesting and innovative presence such as Sepultura or Rancid there are a thousand mediocre opportunists cynically exploiting this new teenage phenomenon. You won't see too many of the pubescent middle-class kids who've been suckered into believing that Green Day or Blink 182 are punks showing up for the adult rough and tumble of violent moshing that goes on at covert thugcore basement gigs in Miami and New York, where those on the fringes of punk society gather to beat the living daylights out of one another.

America now abounds with corporate "tough guy" bands (known as such within the industry) using the rhetoric of mosh pit life in much the same way that commercial R'n'B has exploited menacing hiphop beats, style, and rhetoric. Many of the cultural borrowings of both real mosh pit culture and its corporate parasites owe everything to hip hop. Which is ironic,

6

for hip hop was fundamentally challenging the relevance of rock'n'roll until the moshers reclaimed the territory, and the most powerful pit bands proved that there was life in the old warhorse yet.

The Garden Of Serenity

Gerard works in banking in the City of London. During the day he sports a Ralph Lauren suit and stares at a computer screen. He is vague about exactly what it is that he does, not because he is embarrassed by his job but because most of the guys he knows in the pit wouldn't have a clue what that job was anyway. "It's not like I have a great job," he laughs, "in fact it is shitty and boring but I don't give a fuck. I work so that I have enough money for going to gigs. Buying CDs. Clothes."

The job may be a big nothing but when it comes to music he operates with an obsessive passion. In a town where I can't find more than one or two punk gigs to go to each week, he seems to find five or six. He makes it to all the obvious places, The Garage, The Monarch, The Red Eye, small club and pub venues where you can sometimes catch five band gigs by semi-obscure and on-the-up acts but he also knows about other gigs way out of town that he discovers through photocopied flyers and via a circle of off-the-map fanatics who keep each other informed via the Internet. There are various mailing lists to which Gerard subscribes, and he gets news of things by word of mouth all day on his mobile. Often when I'm talking with him he'll get a call from somebody telling him about a punk all dayer in Paris or an anarchist fund-raiser in some dodgy pub down the East End. I first met him at the

Anarchist Book Fair where he gave me a lecture on the liberating nature of punk.

I find it extraordinarily difficult to imagine Gerard in his suit. He is nineteen and looks a lot younger. For the first six months that I knew him we never spoke but we were the best of friends. We tended to meet at the smaller gigs where we had to help each other out on many occasions before we ever talked. He stood out in the pit, tall, wiry, sarcastic. Sometimes in the pit the two of us would be watching somebody doing something stupid. We'd catch each other's eye and Gerard would condescendingly shrug his shoulders, implying that we were in a world of fools. He subsequently told me that he was glad to run into me because, most of the time, he felt he was "swimming against idiots" in the pit.

Every three or four weeks we'd literally bump into one another or lean on one another to steady ourselves, to take a rest in the combat zone. I *did* get to know him in the pit, despite the fact that our relationship was formed through a sort of rough mime. There were all manner of silent communications. Sometimes a smile. Sometimes an encouraging pat on the shoulder. He seemed to be a good lad.

Gerard frowns on the bigger gigs but he'll follow some underground bands as they start climbing the ladder towards the stadiums. He disapproves of stadium rock not because he likes being on the avant garde cutting edge or because he feels that his heroes are selling out on some nebulous principles of punk.

"I like to mosh. I like the violence. I like the violation of the pit. I don't socialise too much. Most of my time is taken up with my job and the evenings I'm travelling to a gig. Sunday I often don't have too much to do so, of course, I try to have sex on Sundays when the opportunity arises. I don't like to hang out with nobody too much. But I like to hang out in the pit. It's nice to see some of

the pit guys afterwards for sure but I don't even want to get too close to them.

"I'm not from London. My family live out of town but I came here to live because I knew I could have a certain anonymity here. I could earn good money in the City and if I kept to myself I could spend every penny of that money on music. The reason I prefer the small gigs is because there is room to breathe in the pit. You can actually move your arms and legs so that you can duck and dive to avoid punches and kicks. You can dance. They call dancing all kinds of things and older people can't understand it when you tell them moshing can be dancing. Then, nobody can ever recognise dancing until you explain it to them. If you're reasonably fit and young in a spread out pit you'll never get badly touched. You'll just attain a sort of invisibility in there which is a real nice feeling. It's like in those war movies when some stupid pacifist cunt is caught in the front-line and everything seems to be happening around him in slow motion and all he can hear in his fucking ears is classical music and see some image of his virgin girlfriend back home in Paris or London or wherever the fuck he is supposed to come from. And then in the movie of course the next thing you know you see his brain being splattered all over the ground by a random bullet. Well, the part of that where he's hearing the classical music and thinking about his bitch, that's what the pit is like. I don't think you have a conventional awareness of the music at that point. It is part of the experience along with your own body and the shapes that are forming themselves around you. But the pit can be like the bullet splattering your head bit too. Sometimes you snap right out of it because you're about to get a boot on the side of the head . . . But when the pit is cool this is rarely the end of the world, you shouldn't be thinking about enemies when you're in the pit. You're with friends."

The last time I saw Gerard was at Sick Of It All at the Electric Ballroom in Camden. The support act was 28 Days, an ugly-sounding Australian punk outfit who're frowned upon back home as a kid's band but who seemed to be enjoying a fair level of respect in London. They delivered a fine celebratory brand of take-no-prisoners noise which encouraged the pit bulls to bite lumps out of each other. They have a convincing line in punk rhetoric delivered through passionate and subtle two-minute classics like 'Never Give Up' and 'The Bird'.

I liked what they were at so I spent the entire 28 Days set up front with a mixed crew of normal enough kids peppered with 300 pound monsters and the occasional well toned greyhound like Gerard. 28 Days won over the crowd so it was a pleasant pit. The big guys were being smart about it all, and space was being made for girls and little guys.

During the break I headed for the upstairs lounge with Gerard. The talk started, as it often did, with mosh war stories from battles long ago. He was dressed immaculately in Criminal Damage trousers, Vans trainers, and a Mambo hoodie. "I'm really looking forward to Sick Of It All. I love the hard edge sound and I always like their pit," Gerard said. "I like the pain of a rough pit. I get off on it. Not because I want to get hurt all the time . . . just that I like a little pain." He inadvertently pauses to stroke his left eye, which betrays the last remains of a black eye which he got two weeks back. He is about six foot tall, powerfully built but thin, the very essence of teenage good health. He has a certain amount of scarification on his neck.

He says his real motivation for being in the pit is to be involved in the music.

"I love the music. I love the drums and the guitars. Sometimes the lyrics can be totally stupid and say nothing to me but the drums in particular speak volumes to me. So I'm standing there in the darkness and all the lights are focused onto the stage. All I can hear inside my head is the drumming. If the drumming is shit I

11

don't like it and I'm out of there. If the drumming is shit then it's unlikely that there'll be a pit in any case. So I forget about every-thing else. My job, whether the band are cunts, whether the other people in the pit with me are idiots.

"I go off into this other place as I dance and move and touch up against everybody all the time. It is very very sensual. If I've smoked a little beforehand and the drumming is in synch with the band and the pit I lose actual sight of everything around me. Things get a bit darker than they actually are and the only part of myself that I'm aware of is of my body moving like its a musical instrument being played by me and the band. The Ramones have this song I heard one time called 'The Garden Of Serenity' and that is exactly where I feel myself to be when the music and moshing rises to a peak inside me. It is as pleasant as if I'm in a garden full of roses and water fountains where the sun is shining real bright. It's like going on a holiday or having sex. I feel really warm, confident, relaxed. Then of course you snap out of it and you realise you're in some shitty rock club where your feet are stick-ing to the floor and surrounded by their huge sweating monsters and you're a sort of a sweating monster yourself. The garden has disappeared for you but it always comes back again.

"I don't work out. I guess at this age I don't need to but in any case I go moshing at least . . . at least four nights a week. I get the right kind of total body exercise in the pit. To watch out for your-self in there you actually need to be incredibly fit and tight. I've never been as confident of myself as I have been in the pit."

By the time we got back downstairs there had been a substan-tial demographic change in the people gathered around the stage. The entire hall was rammed and sweaty but down around the pit there was hardly room to breathe. Most of the rainbow nation of youth, women, and racial minorities had disappeared, replaced by a monolithic bevy of six foot adult men – aged between twenty and thirty – most of whom weighed in heavy. They were a fit and healthy crew. Friendly enough in their own macho punk way. The vast majority were dressed in jeans and black T-shirts. They had either tight cropped hair, skinheads, or baldheads.

Gerard said he didn't think he'd have much fun in the pit when it was crushed that way. He said he'd come back later to see if it'd loosened up a bit, that he was going to position himself more towards the centre of the hall. This surprised me a lot because I know him to be a fearless defender of his space in the pit. He's not exactly scared of big guys. I asked him why he was going back and he said that it was just going to be too much hassle up front.

"I've seen Sick Of It All three times," he explained, "always in clubs that took about five hundred people. Now that they're playing these ballroom places some of the fun has gone out of it for me. I still love the band, that's why I'm here. But guys like these ones at the front have an attitude, they think they own the space, that because they're adults they have some kind of rights to the pit. It's real fucking grown-up thinking. This kind of *I've worked hard for a living and I'm entitled to my rights* anal bullshit." With that he gave me a high five and ambled elegantly into the crowd where he disappeared at the exact same moment that the lights dimmed and I turned my attention to the stage where Sick Of It All were making their entrance amid an eruption of primitive chaos.

Sick Of It All have been doing their raucous thing for fifteen years and their performance is a well-oiled machine. Not too slick, just a powerful engine of intelligent noise. For the next hour that noise is relentless so there's no way you could call the pit activities a garden of sobriety. A concrete jungle of discord, perhaps. I was not unhappy in there because, while there were big tough guys all around me, there was room enough to manoeuvre and people were respectful of one another. There were kids standing a bit back from the pit, assessing just what sort of welcome they could hope to get. When they saw that it was friendly some of the younger, more loose limbed ones returned. A combination of Sick Of It All's fancy pulsating hardcore and the sheer physical exhaustion that was slowing down the older, bigger moshers calmed down the fury just enough for dancing, rather than fighting, to become the dominant thing.

It took me two days to recover from the muscular strain of surviving that pit. As I left the ballroom I bumped into Gerard. He was as sweaty and as worn out as I was. It turned out that he was one of those who'd re-entered the pit when it'd calmed down. Just that he was working his end and I was working mine so we never saw each other. He was well pleased with the night's excitement but he had to rush off. Work in the morning. What was he doing the following night, a Saturday? "I'm off to Brighton," he grinned. "There's this real good band there called Guts And Education who're organising a squat party. I want to check them out. They've done a couple of singles and tapes they've put together themselves. I'll tell you all about it next time I see you."

White Riot – Woodstock '99

Woodstock '99 shocked America and gave it a wake-up call as stark as that which the original festival gave in '69. The new message was that the kids were turning weird, getting involved in something bizarre beyond the grasp of their parents. But whereas the hippies had been interested in making love, the '99 kids were only interested in making war.

Woodstock '99 took place in an upstate New York small town called Rome, population 10,000. Rome, a typically conservative backwater, is 100 miles away from the site of the original Woodstock. The choice of the disused Griffiss Airport Base, deserted by the US Air Force four years earlier, as a site for a festival associated in the public imagination with love and peace seemed ironic. Perhaps some of the bad vibes left behind by the old war machine clung to the site.

Until film producer and original Woodstock guru Michael Lang started waving greenback dollars in the faces of local entrepreneurs managing the site – the Griffiss Local Development Corporation – the idea had been to turn the airport into an information age business park. Ralph Eannace, County Executive, told a press conference during the festival: "The economic impact is going to unfold as we go along from here. Already in the bank from the Woodstock organisation is one million dollars of host fee, three-quarters of which is going to

15

the rebuilding of the Griffiss base. And the rest is going to the city and county."

Woodstock '99 featured a strong roster of mosh friendly rock bands (Korn, Red Hot Chili Peppers, Buckcherry, Rage Against The Machine, The Offspring) totally in synch with the way things were going out there in young America. In terms of star appeal it was in many ways superior to the somewhat dull array of guitar heroes whose nascent cock rock dominated the original '69 event. Lang made very little space for the hip-hop rebels who, for the last ten years, had defined the cutting edge of both black and white music. In fact the dance acts on offer – Moby, The Chemical Brothers and Fatboy Slim – were just about as white and unadventurous as it is possible to imagine. It is certainly the case that the vast majority of the Woodstock '99 rap metal and nu-metal bands were the fodder monotonously served up on a daily basis on MTV and that this was a white festival for white kids.

The media eventually called it Boobstock, Partydowndude-stock, Rapestock, and Tittystock, claiming that everyone involved was trashing a tradition in the name of Woodstock. "By the time they got to Woodstock it was gone," declared one paper. *Village Voice* related: "Eight cases of rape and sexual assault, allegedly occurring both in and out of the pit, have been reported by the New York State Police – Rome city police indicted a 26-year-old state prison guard, for assaulting a 15-year-old in the concert's final hours."

On July 23 around 200,000 of America's finest youth descended on Smalltown, USA, where they were corralled within a four and a half mile perimeter fence. "It was like a concentration camp," one of them later whined, obviously unaware of what conditions were like in Belsen and Dachau. Inside that fence the police, because it was felt that they would be a provocative presence, were barred until the end of the third day when rioting got so out of hand that baton-wielding cops confronted rioting and looting kids in the only scenes at Woodstock '99 which were truly reminiscent of the Sixties. A month after the riots organisers claimed that ticket sales for the event were actually 187,000. Many felt that this figure was conveniently below the 200,000 mark because, if attendance had gone above that reckoning, the Griffiss Local Development Corporation would have received an additional quarter of a million dollars in accordance with the deal they'd made with Lang and partners.

There were immediate problems on day one caused by the amounts of rubbish and excrement generated by this party army. After using the toilets on-site one local reporter told the BBC: "I was gagging. It was so disgusting. I have never been so grossed out." Another witness said: "I had to go to the bathroom so I went into one of those Porta-Sans. Forget about it. You never saw anything so disgusting in your life. I mean, think of the most disgusting thing you've ever seen and multiply it by a thousand and that's what it was like. I could hardly go."

Lisa Law, a veteran of the original Woodstock, went through the crowd trying to distribute plastic rubbish bags to the festival goers so they could clean up their own mess. Law told the BBC that they told her: "You clean it up. I paid $150." Law said that the attitude of the crowd gathered to hear the Nineties superstars was: "These kids didn't give a shit. *Party! Get down! Fuckin' Yeah!* You know?" Singer-songwriter Alanis Morissette was pelted with shoes and rubbish, and most female performers were subjected to the coarsest of sexist comments.

An atmosphere of claustrophobic sexism permeated the event from the very start with banners held aloft declaring "Show us your tits" and "Girls, look at my ring". One of the main generators of this obsessive mentality was the pay-per-view team whose cameras were, for $60, bringing highlights of the festival (tits, violence, music, and more tits) into the homes of those who wanted to catch the festival from the comfort of their lounge. Pay-per-view cameras zoned in on topless women in the crowd and broadcast those images onto huge video screens which could be seen all over the festival site. Ossie Kilkenny, the Irish co-promoter of Woodstock '99, said that the amount of money he made out of it was "all tied up in the multifarious complexities of pay-per-view." The main stage was flanked by two large camera platforms on each side while a huge light tower stood right in the middle of the site, blocking out unimpeded long distance views of the stage, forcing anybody beyond the tower to catch the show on Jumbatron video screens.

Michael Lang said that, just as in '69, the idea was "to liberate them so they can live the way they want to do." It was pricey, though, to live the way you wanted to, and liberating the kids of their money seemed to be the main politics on offer. A bottle of water was $4, a soda $6, hamburgers $8, and small pizzas were $12. One boy commented that there was "no one there to tell you what is right and wrong" and public address systems advised people to keep on drinking water in between taking drugs.

There was a hell of a lot of moshing on day one to good time pop punk bands like The Offspring, whose fans bounced around joyously in the mud and the dirt, flinging garbage and used plastic bottles at one another. What happened during The Offspring couldn't be described as anything other than good-hearted adolescent exuberance although there were the usual injuries. Subsequently the pit was whipped into a darker, more fanatical and driven state when Korn's somewhat moronic fans replaced the reasonably smart Offspring followers. Korn fans are notoriously obsessive, and they take shows by their heroes very seriously indeed. The injuries mounted but, in terms of what goes on, it was nothing extraordinary.

Each night in the camping area there was an all-night rave

which deprived everyone, especially those who liked their guitar rock and were against the whole nature of the rave sound, of a good night's sleep. By the time the real riots started on the final day, Sunday, a lot of people had not slept for three nights.

The raves were a focus of still more of the sexism at the core of '99. When Korn left the stage it was getting late and the main stage bands were winding down. A lot of Korn's mud caked testosterone-fuelled fans made their way to the rave area where the party began all over again. While one DJ was doing a techno set two women climbed on top of men's shoulders and peeled off their tops. Men swarmed around them, shining flashlights on their breasts and staring hungrily at them like they've never seen tits before. Some of them pulled out their cameras and took a few shots. Then they stood around and looked some more.

Salon magazine reported:

> *"On the pavement outside the rave stage and the movie building a dozen kids have overturned metal garbage cans. They beat on them with sticks with a pulsing, arrhythmic clang. One guy is clearly motivated by the drang. He's shirtless, and has a braided leather belt cinched around his neck. His black hair mats to his forehead and blood, sweat and filth are smeared across his torso. Beltless, his shorts are falling down, exposing at least four inches of vertical crack. He circles around the drummers and picks up a garbage can and slams it into the pavement, baring his teeth and grinning like an overgrown toddler enamored with a rubber ball that won't bounce."*

The Woodstock mood began to change late the following day when Limp Bizkit, infamous for their provocative behaviour, started on the main stage. The crowd had been surly all day. Five hours before Limp Bizkit played one of the blue-shirted medical team told a reporter: "People are really giving us a hard time. I'm stationed down by the light tower. They throw shit at us, steal our stuff. We had to take a woman out yesterday. I'm pretty sure her neck was broken. You can tell because her hands were starting to curl up. Her heart rate was almost non-existent and she was hardly breathing. Her boyfriend didn't want to let her go. I can't wait for Metallica tonight."

During Limp Bizkit, who have taken over rap and made it safe for Mid-western jocks, fans began to dismantle the barriers around MTV's broadcast towers and use the wood as platforms for crowd surfing. Singer Fred Durst told the pit that, "There are no rules" and ordered them to "smash stuff". Thus incited, the pit turned into a serious war zone where vicious guys began to kick the shit out of each other. Bodies on cardboard stretchers emerged from the audience at least twice during every song. Durst was to be seen crowd surfing on one of the pieces of looted corporate wood.

Michael Lang commented: "I think he got dangerously close to inciting people beyond a safe situation." At the end of the Limp Bizkit set an announcement from the stage urged calm: "Please, there are people hurt out there. They are your brothers and sisters. They are under the towers. Please help the medical team get them out of there . . . We have a really serious situation out there." One beefy guy was overheard saying to another Beavis and Butthead mammoth: "Dude, you figure the pit is the closest thing to assault and battery you're going to get without getting arrested."

During the Limp Bizkit set a 24-year-old Pittsburgh woman was stripped, pulled down from the crowd, raped, then surfed to security. Police later said: "Due to the congestion of the crowd she felt that if she yelled for help or fought, she feared she was going to be beaten."

"No perpetrator has been identified and we have no suspects, we have not received tips from anyone," said one cop investigating the incident.

David Schneider, a rehabilitation counsellor working as a volunteer told the *Washington Post* that he saw women being pulled into the pit and having their clothes removed before being assaulted and raped by men in the crowd. "They were pushed in against their will and really raped," Schneider recalled. "From my vantage point it looked like initially there was a struggle and after that there were other people holding them down. It seemed like most of the crowd around were cheering them on."

At one photo booth, a big trailer, guys were lining up to buy film and disposable cameras. Women were standing on top of the trailer, stripping away halter tops and T-shirts. Down on the ground, men were backing away from the trailer to catch a few shots with their disposable cameras. The trailer was providing a one-hour processing service.

On July 25, the third and final day, all hell broke loose. In an example of Sixties cultural arrogance, the organisers decided to put on a candle-lit evening tribute to Jimi Hendrix. They gave out a candle to almost each and every member of an already disgruntled crowd of youths who held Sixties values and icons in complete contempt. During the Hendrix tribute the kids daydreamed about what best to do with their lit candles. They decided to start bonfires and soon the entire airbase was going up in flames. Post-apocalyptic images of raw male torsos, buildings being torn apart, and smoke and flames were broadcast into people's homes via pay-per-view. Some of the garbage fires were 40 feet wide and 20 feet tall.

Five gig attendees and two troopers were injured, one of them seriously, when a trailer was toppled over onto them. Rioters used equipment, cooking oil, gas cylinders and vendors booths as fuel. It looked like the darkest moments from *Apocalypse Now*. They were breaking into payphones, tearing down a three mile long "Peace Walk". Light stands and speaker towers were toppled and smashed. A mob tried to destroy a radio station truck. The biggest fires and the real trouble erupted during, but not because of, The Red Hot Chili Peppers' set. According to *LA Magazine* the Peppers "got stuck with the cheque Durst left".

The rioters' shining hour came when they spotted, and torched, a large fleet of huge articulated lorries located near the perimeter fence. According to Michael Lang: "It spread from one trailer to the next and pretty soon twelve trailers were blazing. This huge incredible image of people dancing around a pyre . . ." It *was* a remarkably poetic form of male violence. The following day the image appeared on TV screens all over the world, ensuring that Woodstock was, once more, a zeitgeist of the times we live in.

The much-maligned Peace Patrol, Woodstock's under–trained security staff, had earlier been accused of encouraging the sexism in the pit, while not taking accusations of sexual harassment seriously. When the rioting started they did next to nothing to control the situation. Transcripts of security walkie-talkie communications were disclosed in the press. "Let it burn . . . Get out!" urged one security supervisor. In another tape a security guard told HQ: "I'm getting my ass kicked out here." The advice he got from his supervisor was, "Kid, go home. Take the security shirt off and walk away. They don't pay enough. Pull out. Let it burn. Let 'em trash it. Get out."

Spin magazine reported: "the vastly outnumbered security force unsuccessfully attempting to quell the chaos and ultimately giving up as fires and looting sprouted across the trash-strewn landscape."

"Pull your fucking people out of there. Get 'em out. What are you trying to stop it for?" said one exasperated security supervisor. "All units abandon! All units abandon!"

It shouldn't have come as such a big surprise. The clear marketing implication behind Woodstock '99 had been that it was the first such festival since '69. In reality there was also a Woodstock '94 featuring a typical bill of hard-line rock acts, organised by Michael Lang. It too ended mired down in violence and controversy originating in the mosh pits.

Woodstock '94 took place on a Catskills farm that ended up looking like it'd been hit by a hurricane. One reporter said that in the aftermath it seemed that the farm had been the site of an uprising. "While music shreds the airwaves," one attendee reported in an online diary, "sweaty bodies slam and bang into each other. They catapult off stages into jerking frenzied masses." Bumps, bruises, bloody noses and broken bones were trophies displayed with pride by the well toned and tattooed mohawk youths who were the Woodstock '94 generation. Betraying a musician's indifference to what goes on in the pit, Blind Melon vocalist Shannon Hoon responded to rumours of three deaths in the crowd by asking the audience to "give them all a big God bless you" before launching into the band's new single. Four thousand '94 Woodstockers sought first aid in the Catskills, while two hundred and fifty were treated at the on-site hospital. The media was being disingenuous when it claimed to be shocked by the '99 riots.

In the vast controversies that emerged in the aftermath of the Woodstock riots, there was scant comment on the alleged rapes and definite violent sexism which characterised the weekend.

The other violence, however, encouraged stimulating commentaries on many aspects of American youth.

Nashville activist Tim Wise, in his critique of the riots, *The Kids Are All-White*, pointed out that the alienation which caused the kids to riot had roots in profoundly white and suburban concerns. How nobody'd picked up the trash. How the toilets were filthy. How they couldn't get a cheap burger. "What happened at Woodstock," Wise declared, "was not a sociopolitical rebellion against corporate greed and expensive foodstuffs (after all these folks thought nothing of forking out $150 for tickets, nor additional hundreds for beer, T-shirts, tattoos, and body piercings)."

This is a fair point but it would be wrong to imply that the Sixties kids rioted because they were opposed to the Vietnam War whereas the Generation X-ers rioted because they were opposed to the price of hamburgers. The kids who've adopted the culture of the mosh pit and the lifestyle of alienation which goes with it exist *inside* society, often living at home with parents and step-parents indifferent to their needs or behaviour. They're not as fortunate as the Sixties hippies; there are no communes, Marrakesh Expresses, or roads to enlightenment down which they can escape. They exist against a landscape strewn with the bodies of gunned-down high school jocks, paraplegic schoolgirls who used to wear Kermit The Frog backpacks, and other victims of an anger which is misunderstood – mistaken for a cretinous lower-middle-class hedonism – by prosperous Baby Boomer commentators.

Tim Wise was, however, right to say that the behaviour of the rioters was yet another example of middle-class white kids getting away with murder in situations where Black and Latino kids would have been crushed. Whenever whites engage in destructive behaviour, Wise claimed, their race is deemed a non-issue, whereas those acts, engaged in by Blacks or Latinos, "bring out the chorus of neo-eugenicists clamouring to explain how there's something either genetic or culturally defective about the swarthier types which causes them to act that way."

Mickey Hart, of The Grateful Dead, the only working artist to play both Woodstocks, told a press conference: "They are screaming just like we were screaming . . . You can say anything in music and its OK. Even if you don't know why you are screaming, you want to outrage your parents. You want to separate yourself from other generations." He recalled that

Woodstock '69 "was not all it was cracked up to be" and that the original festival "was commercial too".

Steve Berlin of Los Lobos, one of the few Old Guy acts to perform at the riot, said: "This is the first generation that's been branded their whole lives. They've been identified as a market opportunity since they took their first breath. And when you take those people and tell them this is going to be culturally and historically important and it turns out to be another commercial, I'd probably get pretty pissed off too."

Fred Durst of Limp Bizkit, who conquered the world on the back of their Woodstock exploits, told the *Washington Post*:

> *"I didn't see anybody getting hurt. You don't see that. When you're looking out on a sea of people and the stage is twenty feet in the air and you're performing and you're feeling your music, how do they expect us to see anything bad going on. Woodstock was about makin' some money and gettin' it in the quickest, easiest way they could get it on and down and done. A lot of people were hurt. A lot of people were scarred for life."*

"They needed someone to point the finger at. They needed a scapegoat." Durst said. "They're not going to put it on the dumb-ass who handed out candles to everybody and said, 'Let's capture a moment. I bet everybody's gonna light them and hold them up.' After these living conditions, after everything that happened, are they gonna burn it down? They're gonna burn it down."

Rage Against The Machine's guitarist Tom Morello recalled that he was only at Woodstock for four or five hours.

> *"My impression of it was sort of through the media's veil. I think that the sexual assaults that occurred were horrific and inexcusable. But, in general, I thought the media coverage was grossly unfair and youth-bashing and tried to vilify an entire generation because of a couple of idiots there. And I thought it was*

ridiculous how they were saying it was this horrible violent event that was a betrayal of the principles of Woodstock. When everyday – whether it's police murders of unarmed citizens or President Clinton's Tomahawk missiles blowing up children's hospitals outside of Belgrade – there are acts of real violence, that are real betrayals of principles, which get one-tenth of the column inches."

Mashing Down Babylon –
A History Of Moshing

The first time that a well-built young man, driven demented by an insane rock sound, stripped to the waist and threw himself recklessly on top of a rock'n'roll crowd, the young man was the singer in the band, not a member of the audience. The guy was Iggy Pop, lead vocalist with The Stooges, and he danced over the crowd, allowing them to shove their index fingers up his asshole, against the backdrop of a band that gave off a dirty aural and spiritual message. Iggy & The Stooges – their first album was 1969's *The Stooges* – were in at the birth of hardcore, punk, and crowd surfing.

From that day to this the history of gig frenzy and band violence has gone hand in hand with frenzied and violent music. When the music has been pretty mellow and conventional, then so too has been the behaviour of the crowd. When the music gets fucked up by the people making it, when that music is loud and proud, then the audience can become a part of both the show and the music. The story of moshing has been the story of extreme music, its extreme practitioners, and the more extreme admirers of that music. But the history of moshing can't be found by looking at any one genre of music – these days they'll mosh to Tony Bennett or Bob Dylan.

The real thing, moshing as a nasty little subculture with its own values and standards of behaviour – as opposed to the reactionary, infantile, and dangerous crowd tornadoes we associate with moshing's current mass popularity – usually takes place in front of live music we call punk or hardcore. In front of those bands who serve up badass music you tend to see badass kids doing reckless and hairy things to one another in the midst of a stampede which has sonic, physical, and spiritual aspects to it.

William Burroughs once said that he thought a punk was "a guy who took it up the ass" and in this, as in other regards, Iggy Pop's performances contained within themselves the very essence of the idea. Iggy reckoned that the Stooges earliest audiences were made up of gays and cripples. He'd originally been a drummer so when he put The Stooges together with his teenage small-town pals he brought his physical grace, his intelligence and his primitive desire into the laying down of primitive rhythm in his band. He later recalled that what he liked about being a singer then was having all that electricity at his disposal. He said he liked to stand in front of the speakers because the power coming out of them moved the air, he liked to feel that air move, and his nightly onstage orgasm derived its primitive allure from the connection between the abstract and the physical. "I wanted music to reach out and strangle people . . . I realised how creepy people are when it comes to listening to something often, at least especially back then. I'm not sure about now. Then it gradually became more and more aggressive until by the time we'd been together six months and we'd not even played a gig yet it was just totally . . . it was assault music."

Stooges guitarist Ron Asheton is on record as saying that the initial attraction for the band to their small following came from "our madness and our own inexperience." He'd seen The Who play Liverpool's Cavern in the mid-Sixties:

"It was my first experience of total pandemonium. It was like a dog pile of people, just trying to grab pieces of Townshend's guitar, and people were scrambling to dive up onstage and he'd swing the guitar at their heads . . . The audience weren't cheering; it was more like animal noises, howling. The whole room turned really primitive – like a pack of starving animals that hadn't eaten in a week and somebody throws a piece of meat. I was afraid. For me it wasn't fun, but it was mesmerising. It was like, 'The plane's burning, the ship's sinking, so lets crush each other.'"

In the early days the Stooges demonic sets went on for as little as half an hour, which was the norm way back then when the gladiatorial aspect of the rock show was still in its infancy. Ashton habitually kept his Marshall stacks at volume 10. When they went into the studios the engineers tried to get them to turn down to eight and a half. The Stooges were the modern opposite of The Rolling Stones, they had no background in the blues or American ethnic music. They were perhaps the first rock band to grow up listening solely to other white rock bands. It was only when they got out on the concert circuit, seeing all these bands doing the blues, that they realised that they had to learn how to do that Chuck Berry rock'n'roll stuff. Ashton says that at the beginning they were regarded as a joke, a clown band with no skills to pay the bills who eventually learned their trade by being onstage.

Iggy's premature crowd surfing and self-injuring antics were part of the music being played. The ex-drummer used his voice and his body as a part of the band's rhythmic assault. He stood on stage in the midst of a wild maelstrom of sound and energy within which he functioned. He just made noises and moved to fit in with the sound. The unique way that the Stooges' guitar and drum sounds were out of kilter with each other established important precedents for all punk bands since then.

Ashton, once described by John Wayne as a "fucking hippy asshole" was taken aback by what Iggy was capable of: "I'd be so wrapped up in seeing what was going on . . . It got to be a little dangerous. *Oh my god, the mike stand has just missed my head. I could get hurt here.* When someone's swinging a mike stand by the end of it and the base of it is a pretty hefty chunk of metal and it just missed your head by an inch . . . The audience was always 'We're so cool. We don't react.' You get them to participate and then they participate too much."

Ashton says that eventually Iggy ritualised and made use of his ability to dive into the crowd.

> *"He got smarter and he used it. He used more of his own sexual gyrations and his athletic ability. It was more of a stage show without having to go into the audience all the time and starting trouble. He would still go in. All the little things he did to them like climbing on their faces and making the swandives off the stage. I used to laugh so hard. This sounds weird but he used to swan dive and the audience knew he was going to dive. 'When's he gonna dive?' In the beginning they were surprised – they'd either be flattened by him or they'd catch him. The next thing was 'When he dives, move.' I'd see a huge crowd and he starts his run and by the time he hits the area it's completely vacant – he'd swan dive into folding chairs and no one's there."*

Scott Asheton, Ron's brother, feels that the Stooges' music was a "sidewinder rattlesnake going through the desert." The music snake mesmerised audiences until they became addicted to the convulsive, offensive, spectacle: "Towards the end of the Stooges all the fun and games turned violent. It got real ugly and dangerous."

Iggy once described a Boston gig supporting Ten Years After as being full of "sexist blues worshippers from the universities." As with all true pioneers, the first man to stage dive and crowd surf found himself to be a man alone that night in Boston:

"So the audience is sitting cross-legged – assuming the 'college' position – right on this huge bare floor. One person in the whole place standing up – ready to hear the concert, right? Ready for class to begin. We weren't exactly the right band to have with this going on. So we come out, right? We come out and start playing. I play our first song. I think it was '1969'. I'm really getting into it, rockin' and reelin' and the guys are playing great. It sounds really great and there was this hush in the audience. It was strange to see that many people quiet . . . I just started the second tune, and beginning with the second tune . . . I began flinging myself at them! Uh, flinging myself on the floor, drawing blood, cutting myself, taunting, but never directly – taunting them and mimicking them, walking amongst them. Finally, after the third song (the club was filled to capacity – 3,000 souls), there was an outburst of applause from about twelve people – still dead silence from the rest."

While the music of The Stooges and that of The Velvet Underground created anything like a punk sensibility, it wasn't until the mid-Seventies emergence of New York punk rock that pogoing, slam dancing, and stage diving – the fundamental components of moshing – came into their own. In London The Sex Pistols, through gigs and the ubiquitous *Great Rock'n'Roll Swindle* movie, presented an image of disaffected and alienated youth doing something that was called dancing but which bore scant resemblance to the free form swaying of the discredited and despised hippies. The very young kids who flocked to see a variety of UK punk bands looked sad, lonely, and beyond the social order. Their dancing, erratic, inelegant, which occasionally resulted in a broken nose or bleeding lips, seemed both extreme and a statement of intent. By the standards of what we observe in the pit today it was a very tame affair.

Luzio, now a London graphic designer but then a fifteen-year-old anarchist from Berlin, travelled to Liverpool to see the Pistols play at Eric's.

"It was kinda full. Not sold out or anything like it but there were a lot of people there. Some of them dressed like punks. Many didn't look like anything special or else they were like longhaired rockers from before punk. Like Neil Young fans. Up the front maybe fifty of the most extreme looking ones – the ones who looked like they'd been hired by Malcolm McClaren to put on some punk theatre – were pogoing violently, smashing into one another, and gobbing at the Pistols. Gobbing, I hated it. It didn't just look so dirty. It was a filthy thing to be doing. I was disgusted when somebody gobbed all over the left shoulder of my new bondage jacket, which was hard to come by in Berlin back then! The other big difference is that today in the mosh pit people can get kind of crushed in on one another. Then they were real spread out and deliberately hostile to each other in that sort of adolescent way. There was a sense of community OK, but it was in the negative rather than a positive sense. There was a little blood spilled as it happened, but you got the idea that, like with the New York punks, there was something a little arty about the statement the Pistols and their slam dancers were trying to make."

The idiot beat of punk rock which inspired the hardcore and punk scenes which exist today came from The Ramones. It would be fair to say that, for young kids in the mid-Seventies, The Ramones gave life itself a kick up the arse. Frank Rynne, front man in Dublin punk band Finger saw The Ramones for the first time in '80.

"When I was fourteen I managed to persuade my folks to let me take two days off school to go to see The Ramones in Dublin. Part of my leverage was that Bob Marley whom they wouldn't let me see the previous year was dead or dying and they'd been passively listening to Ramones for about four years anyway. In Dublin I

went to my brother's flat where I met up with his friends and my art school brother. My own image at that time was a crew cut, combats, or fucked up drainpipe Levis. Army boots and T-shirt and leather jacket. We headed for Phibsboro which was a bit out of town and residential. The bus was full of Ramones goers acting up. There was a good spirit and plenty of punky kids and students.

"Once we got off the bus everywhere you looked the paths and walls were full of skinheads who hated punks at that time. There was an atmosphere of violent threat and a lot of abuse was shouted at us. The gig goers stuck together as we all moved fast towards the venue, an old cinema called The State. This threat solidified the them and us feeling within the crowd because we all knew it would be worse afterwards.

"The bouncers made us all sit down in our allocated seats and my first thought was that there was no way I was going to stay there as, when the lights went out, it was obvious that everyone in the hall was going to charge when the band started. The gang with me all arranged to go over the seats and straight down the centre of the venue. As soon as the lights went out and the gangly shapes appeared to be moving towards instruments everyone ran. By the time Dee Dee was going un du tree faw I was standing in front of Joey on top of the back of a second row cinema seat.

"The entire audience was in or on the front fifteen rows of seats. Pogoing together in a mass. The seats started collapsing and then people went all out to smash them up to get them out of the way. I went through three seats which were then demolished by the mob pogoing. The debris of cushions, bits of cast iron, etc., was passed forward and piled up on the sides or by the barrier so that, by the third song, there was plenty of room for us. I don't know if it was moshing like we have today but everyone was cool with each other, pulling people up and saving them when they went under or when seats broke under them. There was a mass of

tightly crushed pogoing flesh, sexy fun. And going nuts grabbing
for the plectrum showers that happened after every song.

"The crowd were sixteen up, arty types and punks from all over
Ireland. There were cool girls in bondage pants, good looking
boys, some piercings like safety pins in cheeks. Lots of dyed spikey
hair and store-bought bondage pants. After the show the skins
were still there and the next day the papers had the FOUR
STABBED AFTER PUNK GIG headlines. My folks were not
greatly impressed. They ended up reading about it for a week in
the papers. For many years after that there was always that kind
of violence from the skinheads."

The Ramones travelled the world, preaching their anarchic
cartoon hero brand of punk chaos like itinerant minstrels.
Minor Threat/Fugazi leader Ian Mackaye recalls making the
pilgrimage to see them in 1979 in New Haven: "I was a young
fresh-faced punk rocker at the time. I had just seen my first few
bands, it was still a wide-open new world to me."

The new world of possibilities which this fresh faced punk
was exploring in New Haven contained within itself the next
major development in the evolution of punk as a social
movement.

Straight edge, effectively invented by Mackaye, was one of
the most powerful innovations to hit hardcore music and
mosh pit ideology. When people talk of the nobility of the pit,
about the spirit of fraternity to be found there, about the big
vision of how life can be changed through hardcore music,
they're echoing the teenage passions of Ian Mackaye.

During the course of an interview given when he was the
leader of Minor Threat, Mackaye coined the phrase "straight
edge". He said that people should not do drugs, drink alcohol,
smoke, or indulge in casual sex. It is odd that this rather
chaste philosophy caught on in the debauched world of punk
rock but it certainly appealed to large numbers of collegiate

Americans who wanted to be into the radical music but who, in reality, wanted to steer well clear of the more decadent aspects of the culture.

Minor Threat were a clean, lean, and mean punk band flogging a ferocious music and a typically American brand of puritanism. They're one of the few early Eighties American punk bands still selling thousands of records in both the US and abroad. Sleek as greyhounds, Minor Threat's song 'Straight Edge' deals with having better things to do than sitting around fucking up your head, snorting white shit up your nose, and passing out at gigs. Another tune, 'Guilty Of Being White', apologises for a history of race crime, and a third, 'Stand Up', speaks directly to the issue of concert aggression:

> *I came to have a good time,*
> *You came to fight.*
> *But if I do fight*
> *Nothing to fear*
> *'Cause I know my friends are here.*

While founding a major social movement, Mackaye worked at a Haagen-Daz shop in Washington along with his childhood pal – the sometimes celibate and equally puritanical Henry Rollins. When he gave up selling ice cream Mackaye set up the Dischord record label. Minor Threat and subsequently Fugazi issued their records through Dischord, an outfit dedicated to the pure principles of straight edge. Dischord takes ads in zines with a circulation of less than thirty, Fugazi believes in social activism rather than media-grabbing rhetoric. When the band go on the road they choose to book in their gigs using local alternative promoters rather than the rock mafia who are only too happy to book them into the lucrative collegiate/ skatekid circuit where most of their contemporaries clean up. The straight edge symbol is sXe which derives from the old habit in clubs of marking under age attendees of gigs with a marker X to ensure they couldn't get served a drink.

Straight edge, which started life as a minor eccentricity on the fringes of punk's many tribes, has exploded out of all proportion. It has had a profound influence on the rock mainstream, particularly on politically vocal but somewhat po-faced acts like Rage Against The Machine and The Beastie Boys. When Pearl Jam, on their first US national tour, visited Washington Eddie Vedder ordered his flunkies to drive him down to have a look at the bungalow where Mackaye has run his straight edge empire for the last 20 years.

By way of contrast with this mainstream activity, the authentic straight edge movement seems to have gone in many directions at once. On the one hand, it has become a couple-friendly movement, approved of by girlfriends who find straight edge mosh pits profoundly more supportive of women and of communality than other hardcore scenes. Today many straight edge kids are vegans and environmentalists who avoid caffeine and over-the-counter drugs.

There is now a nastier end of the movement which runs counter to the original notion of straight edge being a personal statement, not something to be imposed on others. Vinnie Caruana of New York hardcore band The Movielife reports on the more youth-gang aspect of straight edge: "Sometimes I don't want to be associated with it. There's a lot of kids out there saying they're straight edge and then falling off or beating people up because they're not straight edge and that gives it a bad name. We've run into gangs of hardcore kids at shows just looking to beat people."

It was on the hugely important and violent New York hardcore punk scene that straight edge had it's first influence. Lou Koller, the discreetly straight edge vocalist with New York's militant Sick Of It All recalls the mid-Eighties scene: "Back when we started there was a really raw vibe and a lot of energy. There wasn't really that much trouble. I'm not going to say there weren't any fights, but it was nothing like it got later with gangs of kids attacking people."

Koller reckoned that the media became aware of hardcore at the end of the Eighties. "They liked seeing the tattoos and the crowds going crazy," Koller thinks. "I don't want to blame any one genre but gangsta rap had a lot to do with it. I don't blame gangsta rappers: I blame the kids who listened to it for not being smart enough to understand that those guys are telling stories and not telling you how to live."

Sick Of It All's guitarist Pete Koller recalls: "Back then it was cool to mix the two lifestyles of hardcore and hip hop because hip hop wasn't the trillion-dollar industry that it is now. It started off with beatings, and then escalated to knives, then guns."

"There was this one guy – Dominican Bill," Koller told *Noise Pollution.* "He started off as a really cool kid who loved the music but he was from the Bronx where it was kill or be killed. He started bringing this attitude down to CBGBs. It was things like that – ridiculous things like guns getting pulled – that had them stop hardcore matinees there. Needless to say, later on in life, Bill was shot seven times. The strange thing was he didn't die. But when he got out of hospital the guys who shot him seven times came back and shot him twice. That was that."

At the same time that New York punks were beating the crap out of each other, a word – "mosh" – was rising up to describe this strange vision of communality. Steve Martin, formerly of Agnostic Front, recalls the early Eighties in New York: "I think it came from reggae and ska. I would spell it 'mash' because I would see old ska and reggae records talking about *mashing it up* or *mashing down Babylon.*"

The first band to use the term 'mosh' onstage, between

'81 and '82, were Bad Brains, the multiracial hardcore inno-
vators from Washington. Steve Martin agrees that Bad Brains
facilitated the smooth transfer of the term into punk: "Bad
Brains were the first people I remember using it in that sense.
It would principally have to be Bad Brains, because they were
the first people to bring the punk/reggae fusion that came to
hardcore . . . out of NY hardcore they started talking about
moshing. Because up until then it was called skanking."

"Then," says Martin, "the metal clowns started calling them
'mosh pits', the slow parts where everybody would dance
harder in hardcore songs. When I was playing in Agnostic
Front and I would write a slow part or whatever, those guys
would be like, *Oh, that's a good skank part.* And then the metal
people started calling them mosh parts." The word emerged
into common New York parlance around '83/'84.

Alternatively the term may have been coined by Anthrax or
SOD (Stormtroopers Of Death), an Anthrax affiliated project
whose 'Milano Mosh' was an influential track. New York rock
publicist Trevor Silmser recalls: "What made the word popular
was in '85 this group SOD put out a record and had a song
called 'Milano Mosh' and that was a pretty big crossover
record, basically getting tons of metal kids into hardcore."
Billy Milano from SOD says that although there was a certain
period during which people stopped calling it slamming and
started calling it moshing, it was SOD and not Anthrax that
actually started it.

Scott Ian of Anthrax, who also plays in SOD with Milano,
gives the credit to the more commercial of his two bands:
"The first time I saw moshing at a metal show was when
Anthrax played the old Ritz in early '85 and a pit opened up.
So yeah I can definitely say, as far as I know, we definitely
brought it out into the world of heavy metal. Sadly I would
have to take some responsibility for that."

Dr. Know of Bad Brains says that they had problems

booking gigs because promoters would phone each other advising people not to book the band, whose fans would wreck any venue they got let into. He points out that the moshing which accompanied their gigs was lighthearted. "Nothing got destroyed or anything. In those days it used to be the pogo with the kids just doing the pogo around. That was the dance then, just different, and some people couldn't accept it but the next year it was the in thing and the clubs started booking the bands. But back in them days ain't nobody know what time it was."

By the Nineties Sick Of It All were well known enough to escape the reasonably polite surroundings of New York. On the road they encountered the first signs of the reactionary macho moshing which has beleaguered the American scene from that day to this. "For some reason hardcore music in America attracts a lot of neo-Nazis and white supremacists," says Pete Koller. "One time we played this town in Pennsylvania – it was a real working-class neighbourhood – with Sepultura in '91, and it just exploded into a full-scale riot. We got on stage and they were shouting shit like 'Nigger lovers! Go back to Jew York!' "

In '93, on tour with Biohazard, there was trouble every night, and in Arizona Koller had to jump into the pit to rescue a Mexican kid who was being beaten up. "I think they saw it as something that only white skinheads could be into," Pete recalls. "But we're from New York, y'know? Skinheads in New York are black, Jewish, Asian, anything."

"We played a big show at the Limelight in New York after that," Pete says, "and we made sure that the people who had been our friends in the early days and who we'd seen change didn't get in because there were 3,000 kids there and they're the people who support us. They buy our records, our T-shirts, they pay to get into the shows, and they don't deserve to be beat up by some asshole who gets in for free and who doesn't support the scene."

Then things changed radically – the most important changing of the guard since the original rise of punk happened. Out of Seattle came a wave of rock bands who played no part in the cock-rock circuit on which the likes of Def Leppard and Whitesnake were cleaning up. Nirvana, in particular, became the most commercially successful punk band of all time. Jeff Inman, writing in the *Las Vegas Weekly,* said that, "Suddenly pop culture wasn't dominated by guys just thinking with their Johnsons. Men like Cobain, Eddie Vedder, and Billy Corgan helped rock move up the spinal cord from the crotch to the brain."

Jim Ward of At The Drive-In shared a common feeling that the Nirvana adventure left both musicians and music fans with a twisted vision of where music was taking them: "Our generation is a weird one. We remember being thirteen or fourteen and seeing what happened to Nirvana – when Kurt died. It impacted the way I think about big rock bands."

The mainstream of rock was invaded once more by junkies, layabouts, girly boys, and righteous deviants from the norm. Between '90 and '95 disenfranchised fringe-scene punks wiped out lucrative pomp rock and replaced it with the myriad genres within which mosh pits as we know them emerged and exploded. Hardcore, skacore, grindcore, emo, straight edge, punk, punk pop, were just some of the genres that swamped and replaced cock rock. The New York hardcore No Wave gave rise to The Beastie Boys. The Red Hot Chili Peppers, buff dude bohemian LA kids beleaguered by drug problems, blended hip hop into guitar rock to create the Frankenstein called rap metal. Ministry and The Revolting Cocks took the William Burroughs-inspired sound experiments of Psychic TV and converted them into a fresh and vulgar discipline called Industrial.

LA metal losers Guns 'n Roses blazed a trail across America, rewriting the book on self-destructive behaviour, mayhem marketing, and atrocious behaviour in the mosh pit. After two teenagers were trampled to death at their '88 show at England's Castle Donnington, Axl Rose said:

> *"I saw it go down. Right from the stage. I saw these two faces go up and then go down. They went down and then they came up again and went back down and then they didn't come back up. The audience was going crazy, we brought that out in them. We didn't make 'em do what happened, we stopped the show three times to try to cool things out. The security didn't help. I knew if I went down there there'd be a riot. I think someone could've gone down there and helped those people . . . I don't know what really to think about it."*

On a '91 show in Denver, Colorado Axl stopped the show and insisted that bouncers head into the pit to eject a guy Axl had spotted with a camcorder filming the band. During another '91 show in Missouri an irate Axl dived into the crowd, not to crowd surf, but to capture yet another video camera from a biker by the name of Stump.

Glenn Danzig lead underground mosh pit maestros The Misfits, and Samhain launched death metal-meets-Elvis visionaries Danzig. Produced by Rick Rubin, Danzig released a series of fearless albums backed up by extreme tours of the US, whipping thousands into rough madness. Miami hiphop DJ Karnivore recalls seeing Danzig in Los Angeles in '93:

> *"They had this black Satanic backdrop, the atmosphere was incredibly dark and possessed, the band looked like something out of Kenneth Anger, and the music drove the audience, mainly young wiry guys wearing Slayer and Misfits T-shirts, into a sort of mosh pit I'd never seen before. There was a lot of blood and some guys were laying out some serious punches and drop-kicks. I saw the first signs of that kind of designer moshing, you know? Dudes who'd obviously been practising in front of the mirror.*

> *There were about a thousand at the gig and seventy five per cent*
> *of them were really doing the shit down the front. Including me,*
> *of course, I was there with my Karate Kid moves. It tied in just*
> *fine with the music which was just straight-on rhythm con-*
> *structed out of steel and concrete."*

Spin magazine in '95 reported that moshing itself finally got
the better of Glenn Danzig. The artist H.R. Giger sued Danzig
for unauthorised use of his artwork on band T-shirts. Giger
hired a process server to body surf his way through the mosh
pit to hand deliver legal papers to the singer.

All of these bands filled large auditoriums and sold remarkable numbers of records. But it was Lollapalooza which introduced the concept of an alternative nation of like-minded
youth to a mass audience. Lollapalooza benefited from the
rise and death of Cobain, and from the neoliberalism of the
Clinton era which allowed youth to investigate alternative cultures, protest, and indulge in outright rebellion. Lollapalooza
also wrote the book on what a modern rock festival should be
like. Lots of punk, lots of metal, lots of punk metal, lots of
hardcore, lots of rap metal, and a few Famous Old Guys
(Ramones/Iggy/Dylan) to give the thing a little continuity.
Contemporary rockist triumphs like Reading Festival and the
annual touring Vans mosh and skate fest owe everything to
Lollapalooza. The phenomenon of mass moshing which has
caused injury and death all over the world also has roots in the
behaviour of the vast throngs of people who came to see
Lollapalooza in the early Nineties.

Perry Farrell first conquered the world with Jane's Addiction, a raw blend of drug psychoses and remarkable musician-
ship. From '91 on, Farrell devoted himself to organising the
Lollapalooza travelling festival. Lollapalooza, the word meaning something unknown or outstanding, was originally picked
up from a Three Stooges movie. Bringing together hip

hoppers like The Beastie Boys, Wu Tang Clan, Cypress Hill, old school punks like Rancid, The Ramones and Sonic Youth, and newish innovative acts like Nine Inch Nails, Beck, and Hole, Lollapalooza introduced middle America to hip hop, cultural rhetoric, and the new rock'n'roll.

The original idea was to bring various countercultures into contact with one another on a festival-size bill which toured America. Money was tight back in '91 so, combined with the optimism which grew out of the sudden chart success of Nirvana, the concept of Lollapalooza as a good bargain – Janes Addiction, The Butthole Surfers, Ice-T, and loads of others for a cheap ticket – caught on big time.

As the new style festival battled its way across America throughout the Nineties, the media began to report something new to parents, a remorseless wave of moshing, rioting, and injury in the front rows at Lollapalooza. Suddenly that which until recently was confined to grimy rock dives with a pleasantly disreputable air about them moved into the broad open spaces of sports grounds and fields.

The second Lollapalooza in '92 was headlined by The Red Hot Chili Peppers, then creating a global nation of athletic buff-dude skatekid moshers, and also featured Pearl Jam and Soundgarden. Political sign-up stalls, piercing shacks, and veggie-burger bars were the order of the day.

Lollapalooza '94 saw somebody being paralysed in the pit in Rhode Island during a set by Japanese noiseniks The Boredoms. The ghost of Cobain hung heavily over '94. He'd just died and, up until that death, the intention had been that Nirvana would top the Lollapalooza bill. Nirvana T-shirts were to be seen all through the '94 crowd. Cobain's widow Courtney Love walked through the crowd all friendly and signing autographs.

There was still lots of politics. Families Against Mandatory Sentences were campaigning against sentences of between ten and twenty five years for possession of LSD based on the weight of the paper the acid was on. On the opening night of the tour, before anything happened on the main stage, the mosh pit was large and nasty. Tibetan Monks were greeted with ten minutes of screaming, moshing, and plastic bottles and trash. The Monks' manager came onstage and said, "We thought we'd present the Monks to you because they're an endangered culture. Frankly though, I'm more worried about you."

A remarkable online diary of the Lollapalooza '95 was posted by amongst others, Courtney Love, Beck, and the loquacious and elitist members of Sonic Youth. These guys had good reason to fancy themselves as the arty end of the festival and, despite everything, their postings chronicled a drifting away from any spirit of love, peace and togetherness into a world of sports rock.

Nirvana producer Steve Albini slammed Lollapalooza '95 as a "hoglike spectacle" where the bands were allowing themselves to become the backdrop for a wet T-shirt competition staged by an audience who were "unsupportably crass". Beck reported that "teeming brutes hucked bottles, pants, notebooks, and flaccid condoms onto stage and onto our heads." Beck invited "all muscled upstarts to engage in mutual skull butting to no avail."

Lee Renaldo from Sonic Youth called the moshing he saw during the festival "a passing fancy adopted by jocks and frats in place of wrestling". Ranaldo reported that at the end of Hole's set Courtney Love threw herself into the crowd, only to emerge from the pit topless. Security tried unsuccessfully to cover her as she raised her hands smiling and flipping the bird at the crowd. Renaldo felt that the crowd was divided between:

– shirtless sweating early twenties dudes standing around in groups of three to six, without girlfriends, and

– young teenage girls with faces, clothes, and demeanours

which were the total opposite to the dudes. Not too many of the girls had boyfriends but those who did generally had tame collegiate types who were dubbed "math-boys" by Courtney Love.

As the years went by the festival lost its cutting edge, was accused of booking in dinosaur rock beasts like Metallica and drifting far from the nation of fringe progressive youth that it helped mould. Having taught the masses how to mosh, now the masses were invading the pit, taking it over, and confining the college kid moshers to the side stages.

In '96 Lollapalooza was opened in San Jose by a collection of Shaolin Kung Fu monks from China who got bottled off by gangs of Beavis and Butthead-style rednecks wearing faded Metallica T-shirts. The original vision was getting well blurred. There were roars of approval during the kung fu fighting sequences when endless shouts of "Yeaaah, monks!" and suchlike drowned out the talk on inner peace which accompanied the demonstration. Politics was confined to the "Brain Trough", a small tent which got attention from the jocks because there were free Trojan condoms available there. Some of the deals on offer at the various stalls selling the usual useless trinkets and naff clothes would have made a used-car salesman blush.

Reaz Sacharoff, a 22-year-old slamdancer, speaking in '96, bemoaned the way moshing was going when she said that the pop culture police have been up in arms after this latest counter-cultural threat to society.

> *"It's only now that it's gone mainstream that people are getting hurt because they don't know the rules, let alone the culture that spawned it. Today the 'alternative music' enthusiast who used to look at me dumbfounded when I went into a slam dance wants to mosh to every syrupy pop ballad that the guitarist plays through his distortion pedal."*

Writer Jeff Inman said: "All of a sudden everything is geared toward middle-class suburbanites with too much adrenaline and money."

As the new millennium began, the word "mosh" and the notion of the mosh pit marched unexpectedly into the American mainstream, via the bizarre intervention of some of the country's top right-wing politicians. During the 2000 Republican primaries, everybody from George W. Bush on down ended up being involved in a near-dada moshing controversy. By the early days of 2001 hack journalists were referring to people "jumping into the mosh pit of life", pornographic writers talked of "sexual mosh pits for two", agony aunts were counselling on "marital mosh pits" and political arguments in Congress were being referred to as "verbal mosh pits".

It all started when film-maker and satirist Michael Moore convinced a right-wing family values Presidential candidate Alan Keyes to jump into a portable mosh pit which Moore, supported by a raggle taggle of dreadlocked political veterans from the likes of the Roast Starbucks campaign, dragged from state to state as the Republican primaries progressed. Moore challenged all candidates to "dive in for democracy and body surf the electorate". He said Al Gore should do well in the pit, since it was one of the few walks of life where it was a benefit to be stiff. He thought Vietnam Vet, Senator John McCain, should find the pit a doddle after his famous sojourn in the Hanoi Hilton.

"We will endorse any candidate who jumps in the pit, no questions asked," said Moore. "This has to be the easiest endorsement for any of them to attain. Unlike the way they usually get their backing by taking large sums of money, cutting backroom deals for favours, all we are asking them to do to win our support is simply leap into the outstretched arms of a hundred degenerate – but registered – youth."

In Iowa during January 2000 Moore hauled the mosh pit

around in a large flatbed truck, crisscrossing the state and inviting the candidates to "join the teeming and tattooed masses". The response from the candidates varied. The stunned and frightened multimillionaire Steve Forbes walked briskly by the side of the pit giving it two thumbs up. George Bush shouted at Moore and his moshers to "behave yourself and get a real job".

The moshing farrago came hot on the heels of an event involving Moore wherein Rage Against The Machine forced the New York Stock Exchange to press the alarm button and slam down their steel gates when they showed up with a gang of moshers to do an impromptu performance.

When outraged Republican candidate and right-wing activist Gary Bauer – with the attack on the Stock Exchange very much on his mind – saw Moore and his pit in action in Des Moines he called the local police who sent five cruisers and a paddy wagon to arrest the pit. The police could not contain their laughter when they arrived and saw the group of young adults jumping wildly in place to the music of Rage Against The Machine, many with blue hair and pierced nipples. The police asked the pit to move on, and that was when the trouble and the fun really started.

The pit moved down the street on its truck in the direction of a town hall event being staged by Ronald Reagan's one-time Ambassador to the UN, the black politician and radio show host Alan Keyes. As the truck rolled up in front of the town hall some of Keyes' staff came out to see what all the rumpus was about. When informed that Keyes could get the endorsement of Moore's *The Awful Truth* TV show, Keyes' national field director, displaying traditional Republican can-do, dived right into the pit, hoping that this would grab the endorsement. But the staff were told that the actual candidate would have to jump in if he wanted the endorsement.

Minutes later Keyes emerged from the town hall and,

despite vehement protestations from his Secret Service pro-
tectors, climbed on top of the makeshift stage on the back of
the truck and dived backwards into a howling throbbing mosh
pit. He proceeded to body surf the entire pit – his body carried
like a wave on the outstretched hands of a tightly compacted
crowd. He then did a couple of body slams with a spiked-
haired high school youth before quitting the pit with his tie
still straight. He later said, "One of the folks who was there
looked at me and said, 'You know, you're the only person I've
ever seen dive into a mosh pit and come out with his tie
straight.'" Moore was heard to say that they knew Alan Keyes
was insane, just not how insane he was.

During the subsequent Republican Presidential debate,
which the media described as the defining moment of the
campaign thus far, the likes of Bush and Keyes spent time
arguing and warring about moshing. Reuters called it "surreal".
Future President George W. Bush started the ball rolling when
he turned to Keyes and asked him, "What's it like to be in a
mosh pit?" to which Keyes – obviously on to a winner – replied
"It was a lot of fun actually. I enjoyed it."

Gary Bauer called the profoundly pro-family Keyes – popular
with the Born Again Christian crowd – "anti-family, anti-cop,
and pro-terrorist" because he went moshing to the music of
'The Machine Rages On'. "It's the kind of music," Bauer suggested, "that the killers at Columbine High School were
immersed in."

"Until you told me this fact," Keyes responded, "I had no
idea what that music was. I had nothing to do with that music.
Admittedly I was willing to fall into the mosh pit, but I'll tell
you something. You know why I did that? Because I think that
exemplifies the kind of trust in people that is the heart and
soul of the Keyes campaign . . . And when you trust them, they
will in fact hold you up."

The five hundred media representatives present laughed

uproariously while some of the potential Republican presi-
dents present looked around worriedly. Something was happening and they didn't know what it was. There turned out to
be method to Keyes' madness. The day after his moshing
adventure he scored an unexpected third place finish in the
Iowa caucus. An outsider candidate, the mosh pit incident
gave him his fifteen minutes of fame and fourteen per cent of
the votes.

Now moshing is everywhere. It has reached the stage when
some bands at the more collegiate and cerebral end of the
spectrum, are heartily sick of moshing. None more so than the
Ross Robinson-produced At The Drive-In who were signed to
The Beastie Boys label, Grand Royal. The Beastie Boys, who
once reigned over mosh pits of unbridled raucousness, now
say that, in the mosh pit, real people really do get really badly
hurt.

At The Drive-In tooled themselves way more seriously than
their music (a blend of Janes Addiction, U2 and weird shit)
justified. Nevertheless they were a righteous, remarkably elo-
quent, experiment in post-millennial rock. Lead vocalist
Cedric Bixler, a raucous enough frontman given to throwing
chairs into the air and at TV cameramen, called on his audiences to "shake some ass" and indulged himself in the
demented end of the rock spectrum before he changed his
tune.

"I don't want us to be like fascists or something," he said. "I
really don't think its bad for a band to be hard line about
being nice to each other. Some people just don't get it
though, because they've been force-fed through TV, newspa-
pers and what-not about how to act at a show . . . We grew up
listening to hardcore bands, and punk, and this is what it has
become – slam-dancing mohawks – they had their time and
place. We want to pump new blood into the scene because
there's still a lot of elitism. We're fighting the chauvinistic,

macho brutality that a lot of bands think is OK."

During an *NME*-sponsored gig at London's Astoria in 2001 Bixler ranted at the moshers: "When I was young punk rock used to be about new ideas. If the only way you can express yourselves is to beat the shit out of each other then the counterculture has taught you nothing."

April Long, reviewing them in *NME*, wrote: "At The Drive-In pose a question – can rock'n'roll be saved, or will it die out in the thundering mess of big shorts and Neanderthal violence?"

And somewhere out there on the planet Iggy Pop is still strutting the stage, slutting it up, a hypnotizing desert snake surveying his empire, boys and girls going all feral at the very sight of him. In his fifties he still surfs that crowd, issuing mad teenage cackles when they shove their fingers up his asshole. He still plays the classic old white noise which started the ball rolling thirty something years ago.

Dipping Into The Population –
Hole, Brixton Academy, 1999

On a hot summer night in '99 Hole, the punk rock band led by film star and Kurt Cobain widow Courtney Love, touched down in the Brixton Academy.

The Academy is a rock'n'roll barn holding 5,000 people, a great place to catch a punk rock band or to mosh, pivotal to the emergence of the new music which has rebellion and the spirit of change at its core. The sound of Brixton is the low end rumble of cultures in collision, and the Academy is at the core of that rumble.

Once a cinema, it's the perfect gladiatorial moshing arena because, within the hall, an old-fashioned cinema-style decline leads remorselessly down to the stage and mosh pit. Almost despite yourself, you pick up speed as you approach the pit with a feeling that nothing can stop you now. You're walking through a venerable old pleasure palace with the sense that, like Mad Max, you're leaving polite society far behind you as you approach the post-apocalypse.

The cinema decline encourages a deeply significant aspect of moshing. The younger, fitter, braver crowd go on down the front, compressed in on top of one another, while up behind them the cautious, older, and more spread-out crowd can see everything – the band onstage and the mosh pit erupting. For every brave soul down the front there are two fence-sitters

taking it all in from a safe distance. The attraction is mutual. A
bizarre spectator sport exists for those too old to rock'n'roll
but too young to die while the kids have an audience for their
audacious, weird, extremist behaviour. Kids are seldom terribly weird or extreme without an audience.

Not too long ago a Baptist congregation almost bought the
Academy with a view to converting it into a church. The loss of
a venue of this exact size and elegance – with a progressive
booking policy – would have been a body blow for the emergent hardcore punk and nu-metal scenes. The holy deal fell
through, thank God. Saved from God, the Academy is now
firmly back in the hands of Satan, never more so than on the
night of the Hole gig.

Hole did a soulful and defining gig in front of 5,000 people
who wanted to take home a little bit of Courtney Love, according to herself a walking study in demonology. She brought a
lot of agenda and baggage to the mosh pit. Dowager Empress
of Rock'n'Roll, authentic sex symbol, queen bitch, film star.
The ultimate punk rock girl right up there with Debbie Harry
and Anita Pallenberg. For her young audience she was a heady
mix. A platinum selling husband who'd shot himself through
the head. Touched a hundred times by the hand of heroin.
Many fine influential albums under her belt, the latest being
Celebrity Skin, a controversially radio-friendly classic. Above all,
in this context, an icon for smart young middle-class girls who
are probably giving their nice parents loads to worry about.

Love was extreme, way out there on a psychic limb. Her
skintight skirt stopped just south of her knickers and the
slightest move of her leg, the merest low slung guitar pose,
deliberately revealed those knickers. She was everything an
icon should be, a flaming beacon of art and sex. The people
who saw her that night will always remember her feisty sexuality and the band's phenomenal music. But those near the
stage will have other memories.

She stood right at the very edge of the stage inviting the entire audience to join her onstage. She sang of aching personal loss, all too explicitly mourning the loss of Cobain with tunes about boys on the radio who crash and burn but who fade so slow. Hole in Brixton developed into the most dangerous mosh pit I've ever been in.

Love is famous for her stage diving, pit baiting, and crowd surfing. R.E.M.'s Michael Stipe once said of her that she liked to dip into the population. She came to the discipline relatively late in life. In '91 she saw Mudhoney's Mark Arm stage dive almost every night on tour, casting his tall thin body into the welcoming arms of fans. At London's Astoria she decided to take the plunge herself. Hundreds of hands reached out to grab her but, while they were welcoming, it was not terribly friendly. They groped her, tore off her clothes, and shoved their fingers up her various orifices.

When she finally got back onto the stage she was virtually naked and crying. She delivered a torrent of abuse at the crowd and then, crazed by her experience, smashed her guitar. "It broke into a million pieces," she subsequently told *Siren* magazine. "Like, the full rock thing. I destroyed it. I wasn't thinking. I can be primal. I can do it and not intellectualise breaking my guitar in front of sixteen hundred people – *fuck you!* So many things went wrong, and I was just so mad. I probably did about five thousand dollars worth of damage that night."

The experience haunted her for the longest time and, years later, she posted on the Internet a recollection of her feelings: "I was returned to the stage basically naked, dirty hands had been all over me . . . etc . . . WHAT IS ETC? well it just was etc. I saw a photo of that moment, I was smiling, pretending everything was OK, I guess, it started to dawn on me that this had been my own fault – for bleaching and makeupping and wearing a 'little' dress."

On tour with Nirvana she saw the exact same thing happen to a girl in the audience. In another Internet posting she recalled:

> *"The way I saw the girl being passed around during 'Rape Me' in Ogden Utah from the side of the stage, they were all staring straight ahead . . . as they ripped her shirt, bra, pants – grungey sort of shants actually – panties – as they started mangling her breasts . . . hands on either side – her face was all screwed up in a scream – and the men were all glazed – AND STARING STRAIGHT AHEAD – my eyes followed a particularly violent boob mangling hand down to its owner – a baby faced grunge punque rocquer – at which point I grabbed Novaselic and screamed and pointed – he jumped into the crowd and Kurt had the headlights turned on – I could only point out the cute boy for sure and the girl was bloody and hysterical – her breasts and stomach looked as though she'd been clawed by jackals and Hungry Ghosts, from the coldest hell of the Bardo's."*

When Cobain died in April '94 she didn't spend a great deal of time in isolated mourning. Instead she threw herself into a steady schedule of gigging where her stage diving, her willingness to allow herself to be violated in the pit, was seen in the media as part of her painful efforts to exorcise the ghosts of her husband. She went onstage dressed in widow's rags: "It was fun to play with some of the imagery, to pander to that audience. I got to wear black onstage, which I had never done in my life. And then I worked my thing to death. I put my hair in ringlets every fucking night. I did my Baby-Jane-fuck-you sick thing every fucking night. In Minneapolis I wore a dress that was so restricting, and shoes that were five inches high, I could barely stage dive."

Touring right through the autumn of '94, Love cursed her crowds, spitting water at them and throwing baby dolls into the pit. Most nights she dived into the pit, held aloft by groping hands. Writer Poppy Z. Brite described "her eyes wide and impassive, her limbs stiff as her clothes were shredded and her body battered. Watching Courtney stage dive now was like watching a woman do a painful penance."

In November '95 Love travelled to Orlando, Florida to deal with opportunistic charges brought by two fans who claimed she'd beaten them up in the mosh pit during a show. The judge threw the whole thing out, noting that the fans' injuries were no worse than what one might reasonably expect to incur at "a punk-rock show".

Talking to MTV about her onstage exorcisms, Love explained her rationale: "I think that it's expected that I should go close the drapes and, you know, shoot drugs or something for, you know, five years. But I don't want to do that. You know, I have a baby, I have to make a living . . . it's the one time I feel really good."

When I arrived at the Academy I ran into Mayumi, a somewhat demented hardcore Japanese punk. She was excited to be back in the Academy, a place she loved, and to be seeing Hole, whom she held in the highest esteem. But she launched into a long and coherent diatribe against *Celebrity Skin*, which she said was the work of computer programmers and "assholes like David Geffen". I'd got to know Mayumi in the mosh pit. She shows up all over the place and like many in this crowd, orientates herself towards the world of squat gigs, anarchist punk festivals, and revolutionary politics. But she is not one of the "Courtney killed Kurt" brigade – in fact she thinks Cobain is no great loss – and she can tell the difference between music and ideology, acknowledging that Hole have done a lot of great work.

As I made my way down towards the stage I saw that most of the pierced and tie-died kids around me were, untypically, female. This was pretty much a unique phenomenon. The various genres that give rise to mosh pit action are generally controlled by male bands – bands who discuss at length the male aspects of issues like homo and heterosexuality – and most of the people who come to worship at their various shrines are boys. Hard rock still leans on a certain image of male sexuality. The converse side of this image is an unequivocal attitude towards female sexuality.

Hole draws upon a significantly different crowd; Riot Grrrls, gone wrong suburban princesses who get off on various punk rocks, who idolise elegant women like Patti Smith and Camille Paglia, who share with their male pals a sort of existential weariness. They're nice girls, not necessarily smarter than their male counterparts but way more comfortable with the world of ideas. They're big book readers, demanding and challenging books. The boys tend to express themselves in more primitive ways – in the pit.

Love had at various times brushed up against the neo-feminist Riot Grrrl movement which sought to bring aspects of female sexuality to the fore in the context of rock's ubiquitous sexism. Hole is almost an all-girl band and Love has been associated with certain women-only projects. When nascent Riot Grrrls started showing up at Hole concerts with words like SLUT and BITCH written on their bodies in lipstick, Love wondered if some of the girls fully appreciated the irony of what they were doing, or if they were just being encouraged to look young and harmless. She told *Melody Maker* that she was worried about the fact that the Riot Grrrl scene had become too "teensy, weensy, widdle, cutie. I think the reason the media is so excited about it is because it's saying females are inept, females are naive, females are innocent, clumsy, bratty."

I positioned myself about ten rows back from the barriers which separated fans from the stage. If you actually want to mosh – to move around in a frenzied freedom, kicking, punching, pushing – you need to leave yourself some breathing space, staying a bit away from the actual stage. Stand in the front three or four rows of a big punk gig like this and you're going to get crushed into a dangerous and rigid fulcrum in front of the lead singer, likely to fall to the ground and be crushed under the masses if that rigidly packed arrangement gives way. In the pit, as in life itself, it is best to be free-standing and autonomous.

More and more girls moved into the pit until it became clear that I was going to get crushed anyway. About 1,500 bodies moved into a space where 700 might have been safe if not comfortable. About half the crowd was girls, most of them seventeen or younger, and most of the rest were boys about the same age. With a fair smattering of older types who in the Sixties would have been called Squares. They wore the wrong clothes, gave off the wrong signals, and were presumably drawn in by the tabloid aspects of Love's life. Maybe they just liked good music.

When Hole eventually came on there were instant crowd surges forward, to the left, and to the right. As Mayumi later told me: "Some of these stupid girls spend their evenings online listening to their fucking horrible CD collections. You might as well have dropped them into fucking Vietnam. They were howling, crying, imagining all kinds of shit." I saw one or two girls disappearing under the line of vision only to emerge seconds later, shaken and pale. This was not the kind of audience where anybody was going to be able to help you to your feet again if you were unlucky enough to go down. This was an inexperienced crowd. These girls were profoundly unused to the pit. Reasonably innocuous moments of minor danger frightened the shit out of them. The space I was in was called a mosh pit but the only resemblance it bore to the real thing was its geographical location. Nobody was dancing. A lot of people were not smiling. There was no space for moshing though the valiant efforts of some to construct a zone of their own only added to a confusion which made me want to get out of there right away.

But there was no getting out. I was trapped just like everybody else, caught up in the tyranny of the crowd. All the while Love was onstage flailing her guitar and her fans with incendiary appeals to the kids to go for it. "C'mon! C'mon!" she roared, summoning the crowd onto her stage. Her vexed sexuality whipped the mob into a frenzy.

Having positioned myself for moshing, not for getting crushed, I was in the worst of all possible positions – smack dab in the middle of this dangerous crowd, too far forward to reverse out of the situation, not close enough to the stage barriers either to rely on their solid support or, worst case scenario, be rescued by the bouncers. I had no real control over what direction I was going in but could see all around me dangerous situations where as many as thirty people were toppling in on top of one another. Near-riot conditions prevailed for much of the next couple of hours.

My only advantage was my strength, my familiarity with the terrain, and the endless hours I'd spent in jams like this. The main thing that my experience told me was that I could very easily get killed in there, that it could be difficult to escape. Anti-social though it was, my only hope was to look after Number One.

It took me twenty minutes to fight and claw my way fifteen feet to the very front where, close up against the barriers, I felt safe enough. I spent the next hour catching glimpses of Courtney Love in between trying to protect myself while giving a little assistance to crowd surfers and limp terrified girls who were being passed over my head like a sea of flesh into the arms of a lot of worried looking bouncers.

A German girl right behind me was in a blind terror, unable to breathe, certain that she was about to die. She yelled this to me. In her terror she had forgotten her English but eventually she composed herself sufficiently to scream tearfully to me, "I'm going to die. I'm going to die." At that moment she was not in any particular danger, was hyperventilating rather than failing to breathe, but her state of terror was real enough for all that. I tried to calm her down but she had scant reason to feel calm. Eventually, and it involved an overwhelming effort on the part of myself and two other adult men, we managed to prise her out of the crush and pass her, over our heads, to the security.

In the end, to my relief, the encores were over and the night was over. As Courtney Love bounced so magically from the stage, strips of silver glitter foil fell onto the crowd. It'd been a great gig – certainly one of the best I've ever seen – but I was never so pleased to see a show come to an end in my entire life. There was an extraordinary gusto about Love's reckless goading of the audience but if ever a band should have halted their set until calm was restored, Hole was the band and that was the night. Her goading was legitimate, a powerful statement, but the consequences could have been dire.

During a Hole gig in Sweden a week later – during some of which Courtney Love performed yet another provocative scantily clad set – a 19-year-old girl was crushed to death while several others were badly injured. Love subsequently told the *Toronto Sun*: "I'm really sorry someone died at a festival. Someone, it seems, gets injured or hurt or overdoses or gets squashed at every concert there ever is."

The Civil Service Of Punk –
Vandals, Ataris, Slovenia 2000

New American punk – particularly that sub-genre called jokester punk – is interested in turning a buck.

The Vandals have been around in one form or another since '80. One of the original jokester bands, selling an anarchy burger of schoolkid pranks, John Travolta cover versions, and merchandise, they're pro-active on punk issues such as the shifting of units and the establishing of mail order outlets.

The Vandals, in their own peculiar way, are very Hollywood. They've contributed to the soundtrack of *The X Files*, and to influential neo-punk movies like *Suburbia* and Penelope Spheeris' *Dudes*. They've covered ELO's 'Evil Woman' for a Paramount movie, and 'Summer Loving', from the soundtrack of *Grease*, is the high point of their set.

The Vandals were right in there, along with Green Day and The Offspring, at the re-birth of punk. Whereas the Clinton era saw their pals make it into MTV-crossover heaven and the big halls, The Vandals remain rooted in the more modest circuit of small clubs, nasty moshing, pseudo-fierce stances, and an ideology of touring the world in the back of a van.

Only one member remains from the original line-up, bassist Joe Escalante. Escalante owns King Fu Records, a thriving punk indie putting out albums by young contenders like fast-rising The Ataris. Escalante, an active bullfighter, also operates as a movie producer whose efforts include some straight-to-video releases and *That Darn Punk*, which has a soundtrack featuring The Vandals, The Ataris, and Rancid.

The Vandals *are* a good band. At least one of their songs, 'Marry Me', deserves to be played as long as people listen to punk. It charts true love all the way from youthful lust right through to the rigor mortis and eternal agony of married strife. It is the wittiest punk statement the band ever made, neurotic and distrustful of society's family values. It suggests that people will hang themselves from the family tree, and – a touch of punk misogyny – that for the rest of your wedded life she'll be your awful wedded wife. March '01 saw them in Japan with Offspring. They're signed to Nitro Records which is owned by Dexter Holland of The Offspring.

The Ataris, youngish protégés of The Vandals, are punk favourites in the US, particularly on that jokester circuit dominated by their good buddies Blink 182. Like their mentors, The Ataris keep good influential punk company. They've been variously produced by members of The Vandals, NOFX, and Blink 182.

Formed in 1997, The Ataris put out four albums in their first four years, averaged about 300 gigs a year, and their frontman, the cherubic Kris Roe, got a reputation for being a real nice guy. Not exactly an urban warrior, Roe's parents were hippies who allowed him to quit school at thirteen. After going to see The Vandals play, he passed on a demo to Joe Escalante. Escalante wrote back to Kris offering him a deal on Kung Fu.

The Ataris are that most typical of American phenomena, the shitty little pop group hiding its tawdry commercial ambitions beneath the rhetoric and serious artistic intent of rock, in this case punk rock. Kris Roe writes childish emocore songs which *Kerrang* described as being about "winter days, summer nights, star-gazing, and heartache." *NME* says they're more about pop polish than raw power. Roe wrote one song about preparing a mix tape for a girlfriend and decorating the cassette box with star stickers.

The Ataris, whose audience are borderline pubescent kids, want to play all-age shows and don't want (physical) barriers erected between them and their crowd. They showed where they were coming from when they toured with the incredibly poppy Blink 182. Though Roe says he doesn't want to end up where Blink 182 have ended up (filling indoor arenas and topping charts), this may be his band's fate. They've opened their own shop, Down on Haley, in Santa Barbara. Roe has produced fellow Nitro signing, the Israeli group Useless ID, who're passionate about falafels and nudity.

In 2000 Escalante organised a Kung Fu package tour with The Vandals headlining and The Ataris in support. I caught the tour twice.

At London's Garage, an archetypal nasty old rock club where the security sometimes adopts a hands-off policy, but sometimes doesn't, the gig was promoted by John Curd of *Straight*, London's most significant hardcore punk promoter. He promoted punk from the start, doing early London shows with Blondie and The Clash. He is now Mr. Hardcore. Employing his own rough and ready pit crew, Curd is not scared by the sight of a little blood on the dancefloor. He presided over one of the most violent gigs I've ever been at, by New York's Sick Of It All. That was a boiling night where the men were men and the boys got liquidised. Steam rose from the pit as tough warriors beat the crap out of one another. It was violent but in no sense dangerous. Everyone ended up black and blue but there was no hostile intervention from the bouncers.

The Vandals/Ataris gig reflected Curd's ability to focus in on both band's respective strengths. The Ataris drew a lot of suburban pretty boys busy striking surly poses or disenchanted frowns. These kids preened themselves sulkily in the men's room mirrors before marching out into a mosh-lite pit which involved a fair bit of pushing, shoving, giggling and hopping. Around the edges of this alleged pit, all frowns and disapproving looks, stood The Vandals followers. These were older, drunker, fatter. Men in black, members of the Beergut Mafia.

The days are long gone when you encounter actual original '73/'77 punks in the pit or even on its fringes. The oldest veterans of the pit are rather unpleasant thirtyish types who pursued punk as a fringe activity back in the early Nineties. This Beergut Mafia made up a large part of The Vandals' crowd in London. They saw themselves as founding fathers of the punk revival. As far as they were concerned the music of their youth was the best music ever made, and The Ataris' youngsters were bozos who don't know their arse from their elbow when it comes to real music. They seemed ironically unaware that the very root of punk was the rejection of nostalgia and false sentimentality. The only thing these guys had in common with real punks – then or now – was a cocky, arrogant, high opinion of themselves.

In The Garage the kids reacted well to The Ataris' imprecations to spend money at the merchandise stall. While the younger and better dressed kids gathered in front of the stall where there were obscure releases and T-shirts on sale, The Vandals' veterans took over the pit. This goes on a lot.

When The Vandals started the Beergut Mafia erupted into the most ungainly moshing I've ever seen. These guys were out of condition and too drunk to do anything other than flail their outstretched arms around the place, windmilling into one another, making a big mess as they spilled each other's beers and proceeded to slip and fall onto the wet floor. If there'd been a crowd in the pit it might have been something other than comic. Luckily enough they'd frightened everybody else out of there, and they were falling on top of nobody but themselves. The Ataris addicts gradually returned from their spending sprees and, as the Beergut Mafia rapidly ran out of steam, the little termites gradually worked their way to the front just in time for 'Summer Loving'. One 12-year-old boy with a pink mohawk, his baggy trousers remorselessly slipping off his waist, was held aloft by about 70 boys and girls for an extended solo crowd surf. He must have been up there for 15 minutes. He was howling with innocent laughter. Eventually he went on stage and stage dived, whereupon the whole process started all over again. I think he was a kind of mascot being championed by the other kids. They'd re-taken the pit without much of a struggle. Amusing turf wars are a constant feature of mosh pits.

In early December 2000 the streets of Ljubljana, the capital of Slovenia, were covered with fake bullfighting posters for the Vandals/Ataris gig at Gala Hala in the city's Metelkova squat. All over Ljubljana people involved in underground activities talk about Metelkova, the one-time headquarters of the Yugoslav Army in Slovenia under the Communists. With the fall of Communism the space was taken over by a variety of revolutionary elements. Today this vast site – it once housed the bones of a whole army – is given over to techno clubs, anarchist graphic designers like Stripcore, punk squatters with purple mohawks, straight edged techno anarchists, art galleries, and much else besides.

According to a Metelkova zine, *M'zin,* "The barracks in Metelkova has a symbolic meaning, replacing the pattern of repression and uniformity with the pattern of liberty and diversity."

When the sun set the diversity of Metelkova was not without its threatening aspect. Recently they've persuaded the authorities to turn on the electricity but the exterior was still swamped in a murky darkness, a few bulbs hanging precariously from old lampposts, trees, and the sides of buildings. The warm flickering illumination provided by the numerous bonfires dotted across the landscape was more welcoming. Dogs and children roamed behind huddled groups of adults who look like something out of Dostoyevsky. Dreadlocked boys and girls played bongos around one of the bonfires, punk urchins trying to blag their way into the gig. DJs arrived to play for free before heading off for lucrative gigs elsewhere. There were beer cans everywhere on the ground. The electrics were pretty rudimentary. Power for the gig was being provided by a large old generator situated outside Gala Hala.

What would the kids who hang out at Metelkova, for it was a uniformly youthful punk audience that was queuing to get in, make of jokester punk's capitalist agenda? The circumstances in which our punk heroes now found themselves were by way of sharp contrast with getting tracks onto the *X Files* soundtrack or touring barns with Blink 182.

Getting in proved to be a tedious task. I had to leave the Gala Hala foyer (and ticket desk) and go elsewhere where I purchased a cute looking not-cheap ticket which said the gig was organised by SKUC, a cultural organisation active within Metelkova. The guy selling the ticket, an early thirties longhair wearing a Tortoise T-shirt, stared at me quizzically. When I got back to Gala Hala I joined a well-behaved queue of subdued young punks. They were more like the pretty boy rich kids who came to see The Ataris in London than the ageing booze hounds who liked The Vandals. Five minutes later, no body search or bag inspection, I was inside Gala Hala.

SKUC have roots going well back into the Communist era. They started off in '68 when Ljubljana was the centre of student and radical dissent within Yugoslavia. Art terrorist band Laibach come from near Ljubljana and have been associated with SKUC since its formation. They've done art shows in Gallery SKUC, recorded an album for SKUC, and the name Laibach is an old name for Ljubljana. SKUC operates three separate agendas covering art, music, and revolutionary politics. The music agenda involves the promotion of various types of music but the focus of their efforts is on hardcore punk and metal. They're involved in the national magazine *Rock Vibe* which, despite its naff title, has long been a powerful promoter of hardcore in Slovenia. Back in '93, when all the world was listening to Phil Collins, *Rock Vibe* was writing about Sick Of It All, Sepultura, and Bad Brains. The Vandals have toured Slovenia loads of times, and American hardcore is a big deal there, along with techno and avant garde/experimental.

Gala Hala was a big old military meeting hall, one side of which looked like a tank came through it, causing a wall to collapse. This gaping hole was covered by a huge military green tarpaulin. The crowd was stuffing the space, almost half and half boys and girls.

Every sartorial variation on the punk theme was on display. Lots of elegant 15-year-old kids wearing the exact same expensive sports gear favoured by their New York and London contemporaries; Vans trainers, NOFX sweatshirts, Alphanumeric T-shirts. There was also a similarly teenage but slightly more out-of-town crowd. Their sports gear was made up of crude bootlegs and the occasional Vandals T-shirt. They may have fancied Adidas rock but they didn't own the actual Adidas. These types tended to hang around the back wall and at the sides, somewhat out of place and angsty. They're the very class of people from whose ranks bands and writers usually emerge. The out-of-towners, no matter where they end up in the world, never cease to come from out of town.

At the merchandise stall there was an awesome array of band and Kung Fu gear available. By comparison with all this American rock'n'roll glamour, the hall itself looked bleak or very dated. Not a minimalist black wall or zinc bar in sight. Beer was being sold by the can direct from crates. You could buy a beer if you were ten years old. The air was full of the smell of dope. Almost everybody involved in alternative or youth culture in Slovenia grows their own grass. Other darker drugs find their way in from the East.

There were loads of SKUC guys – bearded philosophical types – on duty inside the hall. They kept in touch with each other through little hand gestures and occasional shouted instructions. They were definitely maintaining a too-close watch on a good-humoured lightweight crowd. The PA was blaring out upful classic punk rock – Sham 69, Ramones, Clash – and the surroundings couldn't have been starker or more appropriate – the crumbling ruins of a dead empire.

Down the front a firmly packed crowd of designer punks and out-of-towners erupted into discordant hopping and dangerous enough punch-filled rolling when The Ataris came on. There was scant stage security so large parts of the pit joined the band onstage, getting good humoured opportunities to play guitar or sing. It looked like quite a triumph for Roe but gradually the crowd kind of switched off. The music, inane enough bubblegum really, didn't make this smart but strange crowd explode into teen mayhem. The pit went off the boil, seemingly pissed off by The Ataris resolute suggestions that, after the set, people should rush off to the merchandise stall to spend. At one stage Roe asked the silent unresponsive crowd: "OK, who's been giving out the Valium? Who's got the Xanex? Own up."

The Vandals enjoyed a bigger success. The mosh pit blew up and loads of the SKUC guys I'd seen all over the place earlier appeared out of nowhere in and around the pit. Despite their Tortoise T-shirts and mellow cool-guy exteriors, they were well able to handle a tough pit, the roughest of whose participants were the bootleg dressed out-of-town kids. The Vandals also plugged the merch vigorously, but this was not what stopped their heaving pit. What did that was the slightly secret police manner of the SKUC security who singled out individual moshers and hassled them until they left the front of stage area. This objectifying of individuals had an insidious effect. It's hard to lose yourself in the noise when some guy who looks like a hip geography teacher is tapping you on the shoulder, frowning, and suggesting that you calm down or quit your space.

There was something terribly wrong about that show. There was a control-freak aspect to the organisers (they even had a security guard on the men's room) which manifested itself once the pit erupted the most, towards the end of The Vandal's set. There were about 70 kids in the pit moshing hard but in a cool and hip way. There must have been about 25 security staff watching them like hawks from every possible vantage point. Meanwhile, the bands, in the extreme cultural context of the squat and its ideals, seemed very shallow or not up to the job. It was like The Monkees, not The Stones, doing Altamont.

The gig ended and the venue emptied quickly. Outside Gala Hala where it was now freezing, the punks stood around the bonfires in small groups, talking bullshit much like their contemporaries back in the West. The chat was about which of the bands was the best, which were the best songs, and how wild the mosh pit was. Not that it had been so very wild. It's just that building yourself up by talking this kind of shit is part of the afterglow of any pit.

Jure, an unshaven boy in his late teens started talking to me. I didn't recall him but he assured me that I was of great help to him in the pit, that I'd rescued him when he was in trouble. I didn't remember ever seeing him before but this happens all the time. You help them out on autopilot. It takes you just a second to reach out and help but, of course, the one in trouble remembers the incident vividly in slow motion. Jure had a heavy baritone which, given how young he looked, made him seem decent and genuine. He had his arm around his bleached blonde girlfriend who spoke poor English. He wore what we in the West would call a thrift store suit the colour of beetroot. After his time in the pit the suit was in need of a pressing. Then I stared at the suit for a second, something clicked, and I remembered his very well from the pit. Things that happen to you in a pressure cooker environment don't necessarily lodge inside in a lateral way. But they do lodge.

Jure ranted and raved about The Ataris whom he thought were a disgrace who "should be put up against a wall and shot by punk police", about the Epitaph label which, he said, "ranked high in the civil service of punk" and SKUC, which is "dominated by pseudo-gurus who look like a cross between Allen Ginsberg and Alexander Solzhenitsyn, who think fucking old. They're terrified of moshing because if anybody had to go to hospital or died, their whole little fantasy that Metelkova is a self-governed anarchist haven would collapse. Suddenly they'd have to deal with the fucking real world like the police, the city officials, insurance companies."

New punk has given a lot of success to a lot of dubious mediocre bands. When you see these jokester bands outside their respective urban Western contexts, you realise how little they have to offer other than cool T-shirts and DVDs. Some audiences, such as the one at Gala Hala, are not as gullible as the mosh pit kids in the West, who are continually duped by the cynical pseudo-revolutionary stances of MTV-friendly charlatans.

Sheer Heart Attack – Musicians On Moshing

Musicians see everything from the stage. Musicians who've had to deal with dead and crushed bodies in their pits clam up or claim they've seen nothing going on from their elevated status as onstage rock superstars. They say that nobody could expect them to be aware of problems such as a hundred people disappearing into a black hole. This is a nasty lie. At any given show the musicians, and the moshers, are the people most aware of what is happening out there in the crowd when it's all going wrong. The bouncers are often focused on rescuing crowd surfers from their own folly and maintaining a holding operation in the middle of the mayhem. Many bouncers, contrary to their supportive body language and rhetoric, are profoundly unsympathetic to the needs and emotions of people in the pit. The musicians have a big advantage – they're elevated above the situation. Usually, they've been out there in that crowd themselves for years; seeing bands as kids, seeing more bands as working musicians, and in certain cases moshing in the pit at their own shows.

I interviewed and talked with a large number of working musicians in the course of my travels through the mosh pit. Most were either amused to be talking about the pit or delighted to have a chance to air their views. When I asked Ishay Berger of Israeli punks Useless ID what he thought about moshing he responded, "I don't think about moshing."

70

That was a good and knowing remark. Defining moshing pointless and Ishay knew it. Not everybody was quite so on the ball.

They turn rebellion into money to the maximum effect in that zone where hardcore and metal blend into a lucrative pit-friendly noise. The new wave of metal acts retains a lot of the arrogance and self-importance associated with the Eighties metal scene. Sometimes talking to major league metal guys is like talking to Hollywood stars; they only want to answer nice or supportive questions. Some of the big players I spoke to on that metal scene, such as Max Cavalera of Soulfly and Andreas Kisser from Sepultura, more or less clammed up, coming on all humourless or monosyllabic, when the subject of moshing came up in conversation. Whereas hipper and younger guys like Joey from Slipknot or Yap from One Minute Silence were more than happy to extol the virtues of the scene, while equally comfortable with acknowledging its bad side.

There is one good reason why the big metal guys might feel the need to clam up. Since the mid-Nineties mosh pit injuries have resulted in more and more legal actions being brought against bands, venues, and promoters. Indeed moshing injuries have replaced the old "My son committed suicide after listening to his favourite band's album played backwards" cases which so plagued old school metal bands before they were wiped out by the new boys. Nevertheless, there is on the part of some musicians an obvious attitude of indifference towards the fate of their fans. I found that the more a band had an art or intellectual interface within their own work, the more they were willing to wax lyrical on moshing.

One acute and challenging band who get to play to the big crowds are Texas rockers And They Will Know Us By Our Trail Of Dead, popularly known these days as Trail Of Dead. They take the concept of concert-as-ritual just about as seriously as you can take it. Maestros of the big stage but willing to work with any size of platform, their shows are heavy exorcisms of demons through music. They wallow in a musical and visual chaos created out of whining guitars competing with psycho vocals to drive the crowd demented. Each night concludes in a bedlam of the imagination where drums get smashed, cymbals fly through the air, amps are given a good kicking, and guitars are bounced off the ground.

Neil Busch of Trail Of Dead reckons that moshing is an unbridled and often dangerous form of youthful expression reflecting an inner struggle within kids who're attempting to come to terms with society. Busch who did his anthropology thesis on the rock concert as ceremony, uniquely combines the life of an on-the-road musician with a hefty academic backdrop. Busch says of his researches:

"I began to see the rock concert as a modern form of civic ritual, consisting of timeless elements; a ritualistic space, music, iconography, and symbolism. Presided over by a master of ceremonies. Similar to the church service or parade, a concert is an event that bypasses the confines of pure entertainment. It aims specifically to bring its members together and increase their sense of community solidarity. At first I thought moshing closely resembled a 'rite of passage' or initiation ritual. I drew direct parallels between the act of moshing and coming of age rites from other cultures. In its most basic elements there were several similarities. There was the creation of the distinction between Us and Them. Young members of the community, mostly male, during my first experiences with the dance in the late Eighties, stripped bare so as to distinguish themselves from other members of the group. 'Initiates' then performed the dance in a space defined and surrounded by the non-participants. During the performance, participants moved around the undefined centre of the 'pit', like some great hurricane of youthful exuberance and anger. As members danced they competed with one another but also with the larger community who

defined the boundaries of the dance area. Just as other cultures have dances that retell their histories and myths, moshing retells the story of life as a young person in western society. Members inside the circle's perimeter struggle against one another, the outside world is constantly pushing in on them, exerting pressure on the dancers. This mimics the way most teenagers feel about the adult world; pushng them, pressurising them to grow up."

Myron Workhorse, joint frontman with Workhorse Movement, is a powerful rugged looking guy with a shaved head and a stiletto sharp insight into his crowd. Workhorse Movement were tarred with the rap-metal brush but this hardly did justice to their sonic thrust, which buried itself deep inside your head in a comfortable way. Myron can work himself into a dog-like frenzy onstage, virtually curling up into a ball of fire before exploding onto the crowd. The audience form a circle in front of his band, responding the same to either Myron or Workhorse Movement's other, equally aggressive frontman, Cornbread. Hard to believe, watching him work up into a taut manic state before throwing himself into the welcoming arms of the pit that Myron is a science graduate with a strong inclination towards returning to the groves of academe when music is all over.

When I met up with him the band were touring Europe on a wing and a prayer. Although signed to Roadrunner, who have the likes of Slipknot and Soulfly on their books, Workhorse were going around Europe in a battered old van, without their own sound man, without strong financial tour support from their label. A Roadrunner decision to pull all funding came at the end of the tour where I caught up with Myron and seemed to take the wind out of their sails. The band disintegrated shortly afterwards, despite the fact that Slipknot were threatening to record Workhorse's best known song, 'Keep The Sabbath Dream Alive'. Myron says he is getting something together with the other Workhorse guys.

The first band Myron saw was Judas Priest on the Defenders Of The Faith tour.

> *"I'd never seen anything like it. The stage show was enormous like an Iron Maiden show. They had the beast from the album cover about forty feet tall. I was on Mars. I'd never seen anything like it, I'd never smelled anything like it . . . that concert/pot smell. I was hooked for life. I'd still love to do a track with any of the guys. I wish I could have caught Kiss. We were always touring when they came back around with the make-up and I'd love to see that show."*

Many musicians say they moshed when young but that now it's a young man's game. Others find it difficult to walk into the crowd and mosh because they're identified by kids and get too much hassle. Still others, like B-Real of Cypress Hill, Iggy Pop, and Myron don't suffer from fear of moshing.

> *"Cornbread and I used to go see bands like Sick Of It All or Clutch before we started the band and we lived in the mosh pits. That hasn't changed too much, the only difference is that now it's at our own shows. I was in the pit for every show of the Tattoo The Earth tour. I couldn't help it. There were 20,000 fans going off to our song 'Keep The Sabbath Dream Alive' so Cornbread and I would dive in."*

Neil Busch from Trail Of Dead caught the moshing bug as a young anonymous man in the crowd:

> *"I grew up in Houston Texas, the fourth largest city in the USA (at that time anyway). It had a huge punk rock scene and I was exposed to many of its delights and horrors. At its best it was young passions exploding in frenetic dance and laughter. At its worst it was skinheads kicking kid's heads in for their boots or friends getting shot in the face in parking lots. Within that environment there was a need for release, a release of anxiety*

within a person. In the punk rock scene of the late Eighties and early Nineties that release was the often violent dance of moshing. Though that term I think came much later with the insurgence of metal into our scene. We called it slam dancing.

"I believe I've seen moshing in it's most awe-inspiring and dangerous forms. Fugazi were touring on their second release Margin Walker. *Skinheads were doing double flips off of the ten foot tall PA speaker towers flanking both sides of the stage. The club, The Axiom, was manic with excitement and violence; there was no clear distinction between bystander and dancer. It was a dangerous place to be, no doubt about it. It could have been an image from* Dante's Inferno; *doomed forever to be pierced by spikes and Doc Martens in the dark oven of a club."*

Useless ID have recorded for Phat Wreck Chords and The Vandal's Kung Fu label. They say they do short music for short people and they've had loads of involvement with punks-most-likely-to-succeed The Ataris. Ishay Berger, growing up in Israel, had his first encounters with moshing as a young member of the unknown crowd involved in local punk and hardcore bands.

"The first hardcore punk show I saw live was in Israel at some point in the early Nineties. Most of the local bands were pretty OK then, except for this really great political hardcore band called Nekhei Naatza . . . they broke up since, and most of the people in that band turned out to be really bitchy and dumb grumpy old punks. But I still remember them rocking in the old days. I've seen most of my favourite bands but I'd love to have seen Minor Threat, Conflict, old Chumbawamba, Black Flag. I got to mosh to some of the bands I went to see as a kid. I couldn't explain why. If I could, I probably wouldn't have done it in the first place. In that respect its like many of the things you do that've got to do with the energy and the excitement involved in getting into punk rock."

75

"I don't go moshing anymore," Neil Busch admits. "At one point in my life it was very therapeutic to be covered in sweat and crash into people. I swore I would never be one of those guys who passively stood on the side of the club and drank a beer while watching a band. Not that I am now, but my world view has changed considerably. I believe that one can achieve the same exuberance and release from dancing with friends and not killing one another, possibly more so."

Dave Chavarri of New York Latino metal act Ill Nino, is reassured by looking out at the pit during his band's sets.

> *"Because we have the heavy end to our sound and also the Latino influence, we attract a fair number of women along with men. To some extent our crowds are better balanced than some others. The presence of the women calms things down just a little. That gives you a chance to see what is going on and I really like that. To me looking out at the pit is a personal thing. It is to see the end result of your life's work displaying itself right there in front of you, not a privilege that everybody has. You've got to be grateful for that. I feel that looking into the pit is like reading a book. But a book written by yourself in part. They're the other half of the equation."*

Ishay Berger takes a somewhat romantic view of scanning his crowd: "Sometimes I get to see old faces at local shows and it really warms my heart to see people who have come to see us since '95. I see all the best friends I have and also all these people I got cut loose from. I see them all in front of me when I play our shit, it can be very, very strong. I don't feel anything on stage. I'm just happy to be up there and to have people spitting at us."

Myron from Workhorse Movement feels like the cat who got the cream when he's onstage, especially during the Tattoo The Earth tour where they shared the bill with Slipknot and Soulfly: "It's usually 'I can't believe I'm getting paid to do this for a living.' I have to keep telling myself to pay attention so I don't miss anything. I was a little disappointed in myself for getting so fucked up during some of the bigger tours we started getting on and realizing that there were big blank spots in my head. I think that's why I started taking a lot of photos."

Neil Busch has a romanticised vision of people who come to see Trail Of Dead. He reckons that, in general, they're people who not only wish to see a performance but wish to participate in it.

> *"They're the kind of people who are open to being personally moved by one's performance. In many ways I feel our shows are life affirming to many people. They see the band giving every ounce of energy and passion that we have to the music, thus encouraging similar feelings in themselves. Not that moshing in any way plays a role in this process. In fact, we have been surprised when it does.*
>
> *"When I'm standing there in the spotlight I don't feel like a rock star or an actor, a performer who is portraying a character or a trumped up version of himself. I feel more like a person fulfilling an ancient role of priest, shaman, or spiritual leader for a group of people just as important as myself. I am creating the vehicle through which people are experiencing life at that moment. Music has always been used by man to stop, or drown out, the internal dialogue of the self. Man feels more comfortable becoming part of a greater collective. They lose 'me' and become 'we' or they become 'dance' or 'rock'. Just as meditation attempts to lose the ego so does a concert take the focus from the self and open avenues people would never have considered travelling. That is a long-winded way of saying that it's fun to lose yourself in the music and the people of a concert."*

While musicians who are pro-moshing flinch at the media coverage given to deaths and injuries which get reported after mega-gigs and festivals, they do have the dubious privilege of seeing the bad things that can happen out there. They loathe the trivialisation of their culture, sometimes citing the number of people who get sports or driving injuries every day of the week. Some musicians rightly feel they have a duty to police the pit themselves. "In Detroit there are some skinhead gangs that are at all the heavy shows," Myron Workhorse says, "and they really mess things up for the other kids in the pit because there's five to ten dicks in there that just want to fight and really hurt people. So I have a little bit of a bad attitude towards it because of that but when that element isn't there it's such a ritual."

Frank Rynne of Dublin punk band Finger has worked the arty end of the scene with Richard Hell and Lydia Lunch. He has other reservations about moshing, which he feels are shared by other musicians.

> *"It is a great and potent ritual for sure, but it may yet become a millstone around the necks of those of us who want to make art over money, to put it simply. The problem I have with moshing is that it may very well bring 'The Mob' into your gig, into the world of your band. A big unwanted unruly element who don't give a fuck about your music. As long as the agenda is the agenda I associate with the pit – solidarity amongst peers, a neighbourly attitude, opposition to racism, sexism, homophobia . . . love and understanding of music – I'm happy about it. Then we're all dancing at the same party.*
>
> *"But there is another agenda going on right now, particularly in America and around certain bands. It's a reactionary vibe I associate with a lot of assholes who would claim the right to be in the pit but who have no real place in there. I'm talking about shit like sexual harassment and no-purpose violence. It's always important to remember moshing is primarily a music issue, a process which is ancillary to music, not some sort of street gang gimmick on the fringes of sports metal. I can't stand those*

fucking meatheads who want to mosh and mosh and mosh. They don't want you doing songs which they perceive as being 'slow', they don't want to hear the things you have to say between tunes, they just want heavy fast frantic shit they can mosh to. I love that more than they do so they can fuck off. They don't even know what a 'slow' song is. They should just go to the gym or join the army. Work it out of their system somewhere else with somebody else. Still, when Jack Kerouac referred to the sheer heart attack of life, he may well have had the thrill of moshing in mind."

Bouncers

Bouncers – or security guards – tend to have things easy and to be let off the hook when it comes to looking at the negative aspects of moshing. They stand in the front line between an audience in trouble and the relief they may need from that trouble. It has been my own experience, and the uniform feeling of mosh pit kids with whom I've discussed this, that bouncers maintain an unenviable reputation as a negative presence at most gigs they work at.

They don't just passively allow things to happen. They occasionally make things worse.

> *"I was at Kid Rock and it was a phenomenal pit. It was just about the best fun I ever had at a gig. That was what I felt that night. I guess part of the reason for that was that, at that moment in time, the whole world knew three or four of Kid's songs like 'Cowboy'. I knew the whole album, played it nearly every night so that my Mom knew if off by heart too. And Kid Rock came on and played nothing else except the album. He played every track from it and he did a cover version of some rock classic which I knew too although I don't know the name of it. I think it was Metallica or Black Sabbath.*
>
> *"The fact that we all knew every song made us all real high and made the pit noisy and tough. It was a real feeling of power, like you were invincible. It was a small stage but then had a line*

of tough looking bouncers right across the front like soldiers in a line. They knew it was going to be a busy pit. They dragged exhausted people from the very front but they had a real nasty attitude to surfers. You'd have somebody surfing all the way to the front. They'd be excited and hyper with themselves. Especially when they could see the stage coming up right there in front of them and they knew that soon they'd have reached their goal. Normally the bouncers will move forward to catch you if you're surfing. Then take you to the side of the stage where you can usually get a drink of water before heading back to the pit. I was watching surfers coming to the front and the bouncers moved forward like to grab them. Then just as the surfers thought they were about to be grabbed and rescued they were pushed back violently into the pit, causing some of them to splat on the floor and more of them to get caught up in the next wave of surfers coming in on top of them. The incoming was fierce. The last thing each and every one of them was expecting was to be pushed back into the pit. They were all caught off balance. I felt it was really not what those guys were being paid to do."

Not all bouncers are bad, it goes without saying. There was a bouncer called Neville who used to work the rock gigs in London when I first started moshing. He was a dreadlocked black guy who always had a smile on his face, who seemed to like moshers, and who was truly welcoming of kids arriving into his arms after suffering the vagaries of the pit. Certain bands, bands that I respected, insisted on Neville being brought out on the road with them to do pit security. You'd see other bouncers working with him, whose personalities varied between – on the one hand – nice guys who were just not as hip as Neville, and – on the other – those who had the dispositions of Attila the Hun. They stared at Neville, who seemed to be handling the hard workload landing on him with grace under pressure, awe-struck by the straightforward friendships which existed between this big black guy and the pit of white scrawny urchins he was helping.

Eventually the Neville method became part and parcel of the approach of many London bouncers. Suddenly the security pit was full of professional Nice Guys – other black guys with dreadlocks and occasional big white guys with rock-style long hair – who came on so very supportive but who, in fact, had hardly changed their bad attitudes at all. Henry, who went to many of those Neville-era shows with me, reckoned that the change was purely cosmetic, that the bouncers in one central London venue, where most upwardly mobile bands wanted to play, were little more than a criminal gang using the venue as a convenient city centre location.

"Up until Neville came along, you were as likely as not to get a punch in the face, far worse than any little scuff you got in the pit, when you dropped into the arms of bouncers at the Writzy. The Writzy was the worst. The bouncers there had a reputation for drug dealing and drug taking. Sometimes when I was close to the front I'd look at some of the bouncers. There was one in particular who had dreadlocks but who was way bigger than Neville. Several nights I saw him with water running out of his eyes while he was on duty, his nose running, him continually rubbing his nose like he'd forgotten where it was located. If you were found with a little bit of dope in your pocket they'd shake you down because they had the concession on dealing in The Writzy.

"I had a friend who usually worked as a criminal and he was trying to go straight so somebody down the East End fixed him up with the bouncer crew that worked at The Writzy. He got in there but he felt they were distrustful of him because he was a pretty capable white guy in his mid-twenties who knew what way the cookie crumbled. They let him in on the E dealing which was where they made their real profits but he felt that the atmosphere was weird, that he'd come to a bad end if he stayed with them. It

was as difficult to get out of his arrangement as it was to get into it in the first place. At the same time there was this other guy who they allowed to deal in the men's toilet on their behalf. They sanctioned him and provided him with supplies. He was a stupid cunt and he ran off with about £4,000 of their money. Nothing happened for a month. Then one day one of the bouncers – this big bloke – was walking through Soho and he saw the guy who'd absconded. He followed the guy discreetly, phoning the other bouncers on his mobile to tell them the good news. They were around at The Rio. They told him to push the guy into a phone booth and keep him there. When he was in the phone booth – he was just this small little gay guy so it was easy to force him into one – the bouncer who trapped him phoned his homies and gave them his location. Ten minutes later they all arrived in a van and took him off to a house somewhere where they stripped him and broke nearly every bone in his body. He lived and recovered more or less but he was in hospital in and out for months."

Neville subsequently died in a motorcycle crash, driving home late one night after a show somewhere. *Kerrang* carried fulsome tributes to him from bands and kids whom he'd helped out. The real point about Neville was not that he was a nice guy – he may well have been – but that his supportive attitude was the exception, not the rule. A nice guy stood out so much because the rest of them were not very nice.

There are two consistent and universal criticisms of bouncers. One concerns their general lack of sympathy for the kids – often white, prosperous, small, very young – who mosh. The other relates to their indifference to sexual assaults which happen in the crowd. There were countless suggestions after Woodstock '99 that the bouncers turned a blind eye to actual rapes they saw happening in front of them. My own experience would lead me to believe that these suggestions sound plausible enough. Time and time again I've seen scared and lonely kids – often in need of nothing more than a comforting word – being rebuffed by bouncers no matter what the problem was. I've seen bouncers refuse to go and get water for dehydrated kids at big open air festivals attended by 50,000. It would be fair to say that, of the maybe five times I've seen people bringing sex attacks to the attention of bouncers, the bouncers have completely ignored the accusations in all but one case. In that one case the security in question were supportive of the alleged victim, and instigated a manhunt through the pit for the alleged attacker. The guy got away but, on that one occasion, security was competent and diligent.

Internet mosh chat rooms are weighed down with serious complaints against security, and most of these complaints concern security refusing to act when told about incidents that deserve attention. One kid attending a Green Day show in California had several sexual approaches made to him by another kid he stumbled across in the pit. I tracked down the kid via his e.mail and he elaborated on his experience.

"I could feel this hand groping my cock. I took it for granted that it was this real cute girl a bit older than me who was in front of me and slightly to my left. After a while I worked out from the fact that I could see both her hands in the air that it couldn't be her. There were some other girls around but their geographical location suggested they were unlikely too. Neither of them looked so good either but that is not the point. I worked out that it was a guy about two years older than me, about eighteen. I worked it out because he was looking at me all the time and smiling at me. Earlier of course I'd smiled back at him while I thought it was the girl . . . so I knew I had myself to blame really. I was pretty damned stoned and he had every reason to think that I was on for it. So I said to him, 'Man, I'm sorry but I'm straight.' He smiled like that was OK and he took away his hand. Then later it was back again so I said it to him, he stopped, then much later I

84

could feel him about to go for it again so I just kind of flipped. I tore through the few people in front of me and approached the first bouncer I saw. I tugged him on the arm and he sort of barked 'What?' at me. I told him there was this guy . . . blah blah blah . . . and he just kind of fixed me with a look like I was filthy or something. He walked away and got some water which he started giving out to the crowd. I grabbed at another one and he didn't even want to hear me. He just kept staring right ahead watching out for surfers. Then I decided to forget the whole fucking thing. I was stoned and now after using up all that energy trying to catch the bouncer's attention I didn't give a fuck anymore. But if I'd had a heart attack or I'd been raped or punched, those guys would have reacted the same way. They were just there to get paid and to drag in the occasional crowd surfer."

I've seen all this stuff and more going on. The whole system of hiring professional security with backgrounds in martial arts and the criminal drug underworld is a global problem. Then again, my own personal encounters with bouncers – bar one very unpleasant incident – have been nothing other than fine. As in every walk of life, there are some very decent people working on that scene amid the thugs.

It is an obvious fact that the majority of bouncers have little sympathy for the culture of rock gigs or their pits. They're seeing, and working through, scenes they must regard as being the very essence of stupidity. Most of them don't like harsh aggressive hardcore music or its fans. There are class, racial, or generational gaps between most bouncers and most people at rock concerts. You do occasionally see, even at quite big and demanding shows, guys from bands working as bouncers. They can be good at the job because they have a feel for the crowd and the milieu.

Pits would be safer and nicer places if front of stage security was made up of well-trained semi-professionals who were ex-

professional musicians, young impoverished musicians, or reasonably astute young men and women from the pit. This may
sound like recklessness and, no doubt, security professionals
would need to be on-site. The current yawning gap which
exists between the attitudes of professional stage security and
moshers is a major part of the problem in moshing today.

Unwelcome Visitors Permitted

Jesus pulled himself out of the pit. That involved a super-human effort. Behind him 800 big guys and the occasional plucky small guy moshed on and on with ferocious violence in front of a New York hardcore band. They'd been rolling with the beat, using their adrenaline-fuelled fists and legs to punch out a space for movement. Only there were 800 of them packed into a space about the size of a big living room so they'd punched each other black and blue.

The rest of the packed hall was equally restive, just that they had more room to move about a little and were not participating in the rituals of the pit. Jesus was getting his rocks off, but now it was time to leave the blitz and head for home.

He stumbled into the nearest convenience store where he bought a load of expensive well-chilled Tropicana fruit juice. As he queued to pay for his juice another sweat drenched guy from the pit, also Latino, came into the store. The kid, sporting a huge black eye, fixed Jesus with a keen amused stare. "Well . . ." he paused for a second, staring at Jesus. "It was quite a time!"

By 3 a.m. Jesus was slumped into a battered old couch in the lounge of the Spanish Harlem apartment he shared with two others, listening to hip hop, recovering from the pit. He had a substantial weal on his right arm, a deep bite mark on his right shoulder. One of his big toes felt like it was broken or, at least, badly bruised. While it was now obvious that neither of his eyes was going to turn black and blue, he had visible lumps on both eyebrows so that it hurt every time he blinked. The sixteen-year-old boy he'd met in the convenience store – Jose – was crashed out in a spare bedroom. A suburban lad, Jose claimed to have missed the last train home but in the big city there is no such thing as the last train. Two hours usually separates the last night train from the first morning one.

The reality was that Jose didn't want the magic and conspiracy of the mosh pit to end after the final encore but the music *was* over. Jesus was the big older guy who'd helped protect Jose during the chaos and tangle of bodies in the pit so it fell to him, a relatively inner city resident, to bring his Latino brother back to his place, feed him, and play him hip-hop records until Jose – a schoolboy in reality – had to crash.

Jesus was older, tougher, and he'd built himself up for staying power. He'd been in mosh pits infinitely more times than Jose although, like all adolescents, Jose regarded himself as being a hardened veteran. Jose thought that Jesus was just like him only older. Earlier in the evening Jose said to Jesus, "What were you like when you was my age? Were you like me?" and Jesus, who went into the pit to be an isolated individual, not to be a part of the gang, replied, "No. I was like me." At 22, Jesus was old enough to realise that he and Jose had absolutely nothing in common other than their love of hardcore punk and their reliance on the pit as a source of fraternity in the lonely city.

Jesus's film student older brother, who lived in the apartment with him, had sprayed a large graffiti on the back wall of the lounge. It read "Unwelcome visitors permitted", apparently a quotation from the writer William Burroughs who'd invented the very phrase Heavy Metal. Sometimes, when he dragged pit survivors home in the middle of the night, Jesus felt that he should nail a sign saying "Unwelcome Visitors Permitted" to his front door.

He nursed his bruises gently, more or less proud of them, enjoying the soft beats of the hip-hop music which seemed, along with the joint he was smoking, to relieve the pain. The pain was as nice as the dope. In the morning Jose would be full of surly, adolescent, embarrassment. Jesus would be busy getting ready for college, the same guy that he was right now. The same guy he'd been in the pit the night before when he gave Jose that black eye.

Surviving The Pit

The only way to find out what a pit is like is to go into one. To go into a pit you need to be in reasonably good condition. It helps to be young and fit. If you're not young, you certainly need to be fit. Even if you are fit, but temporarily discommoded with a minor injury or infection, stay away. You need all your physical and mental abilities about you in there.

While it is not necessary to be smart to survive, it helps, and it is certainly necessary to have substantial street smarts. In the pit you'll encounter people from substantially different milieus from yourself. If you're new to the scene you may find life disconcerting there for a while. You may well be a carefully nurtured product of a nuclear family from out in suburbia, but when you walk into the pit you'll meet people from all layers of society. You may meet those much more experienced in life than yourself. You will meet up with individuals active in drug subcultures and those who like at least the thrill of violence. It is worth noting that some of those violent guys will be good responsible characters who're worth getting to know. A small number are not worth getting to know. But you need to keep a good look out when you go moshing.

Smart or not, you need to remain calm and not freak out. A calm head helps you achieve most of the things you might hope to experience in the pit, such as having a good time. Rock Medicine, a California-based organisation which grew out of the Haight-Ashbury Free Clinic movement, provides supportive medical treatment at rock shows in California. They agree that many of the real problems that happen in the crowd are nothing more than panic attacks.

> *"Many of the people we see at Rock Medicine come in simply because they're so overpowered by the event. What we call 'crowd syndrome' is simply a combination of over-excitement and energy due to the number of people in the crowd, the flashing lights, the loud music, and the heat. If you feel very hot and sweaty, short of breath and faint, you need to get away from it all for a while in a relatively quiet place."*

People need to understand that they're the authors of their own destinies in the pit. It is not a great idea to be too drunk or too stoned if you want to mosh. It remains an unglamorous fact that most of the problems people have at gigs derive from the fact that they've consumed too much, be it drink or drugs. A doctor with Rock Medicine said, when the casualties were coming in hot and heavy at a metal show, that drink was the biggest problem: "Too much, too soon, too late. They drink too much and, before you know it, it's too much." Rock Medicine says that most of their patients come to them due to over-indulgence in some form.

> *"Some are simply overcome by the size of the crowd and the level of energy/excitement. A small minority may be involved in a more serious situation and require repair to a cut. Others need confirmation that they have a possible sprained ankle and should get an X-ray as soon as possible . . . A very small number require transport to a hospital."*

This is borne out by statistics from a triple bill of Metallica, Korn, and Kid Rock which drew 30,000 people to Rockingham, North Carolina, in July 2000. The local hospital released the figures on injuries during the show, which they said were "not nearly the amount" that they'd expected. Eleven were sent to the hospital, four of them had drug/alcohol problems, three suffered orthopaedic injuries such as fractures and sprains, three had lacerations, and one had a peptic ulcer. Thirty five people, who passed out or were feeling weak or not so good, were treated on site, as were, amongst others, fourteen orthopaedic injuries, twelve respiratory problems, five who were assaulted or struck, and three who had seizures.

To survive in the pit, it's important to be at ease with the music that the band are playing. There is nothing worse than the guy in the pit who is there merely to mosh, while knowing little about the repertoire or, sometimes, holding the band in complete contempt. You don't have to regard the given band as godlike presences – many in the pit will have harsh views on their apparent idols – but you've got to be in love with the music enough to have yourself a good time.

Chances are that, that fateful night when you first go moshing, you'll not be the only person taking the dive for the first time. There will be plenty more there who are on their first, second, or third adventure. It seems that the active career of the average mosher is not that long in any case. There exists a hardcore element of lifers who can't get enough of it. They intend moshing right down to the end of the line. But there are many people who only mosh for six to nine months. They then feel they've had the experience, or that they should grow up a bit. Some of those eventually miss the thrill and reintroduce themselves to the phenomenon when they're a little bit older and participate by dipping in occasionally whenever their favourite bands are playing.

If you're a pit virgin, it is worth noting that some pits may provide better opportunities than others. It is a good idea to start with a well attended small club gig. People can watch out for you there and the sense of community in the pit will be in effect. It is also worth paying attention to what genre of music you really want to mosh. I found metal crowds to be the best in terms of generosity of spirit and sense of adventure. A metal pit is a mental pit, there are people in there who are up for anything. It is in metal pits that the sexual aspect of the pit is in play to the maximum extent. It is in metal pits that individuals undergo the most substantial alterations of personality. If you're in the pit at a left-leaning metal band with a strong rhythmic underpinning (like Sepultura or Soulfly) then you are probably safe. You're also reasonably safe at small hardcore shows where the action is heavier but where the psychic payback is incremental. Big punk gigs by real punk bands like Rancid have good pits but are also rough enough.

The worst pits, in terms of uncool behaviour, are undoubtedly those connected with stadium nu-metal and rap-metal. A lot of these bands are the mainstream chart acts of the moment, attracting the largest possible numbers of extremely young fans. Lots of inexperienced younger kids go into pits at these gigs. They're often of an age when they imagine themselves to be tough guys, and they're at the receiving end of an intimidating amount of corporate propaganda which expects them to act up.

The most dangerous aspect of big gigs full of inexperienced kids concerns something which is often called moshing but which is not moshing in any sense of the word, though it may take place proximate to where the pit might be. Crowd surges and crushes are as old as music itself, and happen at religious music festivals in India, during mass visits to Mecca, and at football/sports events all over the world. I've been caught up in many such crushes and surges at gigs, some of the more frightening experiences I've had. There might be 50,000 people extending back into the middle distance, with less than a hundred security guards working from behind the safety of elaborate security barriers right up at the very front.

If you're caught out there in the middle of that crowd when

morons start pushing and shoving forward en masse, you could become very badly unstuck. At gigs that size, when people try to pass by you talking bullshit – during the chaos of a performance – about how their girlfriend/brother/best friend is just up ahead that bit closer to the stage, you have a duty to refuse to let them pass. They're often people more at home in the nightclub environment than in the middle of a gig crowd. They have no sense of the collective danger they're helping to construct. They are generally full of an alcohol-fuelled self-confidence which convinces them that they can dupe people into letting them pass. This makes them in-credibly arrogant and pushy. They think they'll end up front of stage. People owe it to one another to reject this nonsense, which may have had some place at gigs in the past when the pace was that bit slower. Not now.

At an industrial club I met a girl called Catherine who recalled her experiences at a huge gig.

"The last time I saw Marilyn Manson was in a hangar-like shed in Los Angeles. There must have been 15,000 people. I'd not been too much impressed with Manson the last time I'd caught him, which was in a small club when he was right at the height of his notoriety. I ended up that time standing rigidly still in the middle of a thousand very dreary and boring people. All caught up in the cult of their idol. He was doing some Eurythmics song which I hated.

"I went again because my sister needed to go and I wanted to see if he could really deliver a good show. My sister was happy enough to play it safe at the back but I moved towards the front after the second billing guys came off. They were dreadful, I think Manson had some role or other in their careers. I had to negotiate my way through a lot of very cranky and uptight people to get anywhere near the stage, and this was a big tedious deal. There were a lot of romanced-up late teen couples who were suddenly

realizing how very close to one another they were. The guys were all faggy skinny ones wearing black, often with bits of lace and stupid shit. The women weighed in a bit heavier but there were some complete and utter cows amongst them. The couples wouldn't give an inch.

"I got the impression that a lot of them were very routine and mundane people – hairdressers from the burbs and guys who worked at Radio Shack – who were going through their eerie supernatural weirdo phases. Being into Manson for a couple of years before they settled down to baby making. I think Manson's career has suffered a lot from the fact that his shock appeal has died down and there are other freak shows out there. I think he did a lot of good with the way he provoked people. What he had to say was cool enough – in the context of the way America was drifting right then – but the music was always secondary.

By the time he came on with his band I was three quarters of the way towards the front, which was not enough. I thought I'd battle the rest of the way during the first twenty minutes. Normally when the band comes on some people get freaked out and flee to the back of the hall. That and the moshing loosens up some space . . . if you're a part-time mosher like me you'll be able to negotiate your way through the pit most of the time. It didn't happen that night. I couldn't move left or right, back or forward. It was totally fucked up.

"There were lots of frantic girls around me who were hopeless, behaving like Backstreet Boys fans. It was just stupid fanmania. I tried to back out of the situation but that proved impossible. The oafs behind me refused to budge – maybe they couldn't anyway – how can you make a space where there's 15,000 others pushing against you? I got really worried, I knew this was a not good situation. I was not what somebody called a happy item. The psychological feeling was like being out at sea, the water coming up to your neck. Elsewhere I could see the entire crowd swaying with small numbers collapsing in on each other. Then Manson did

some well known song – I was way too bothered to notice which one – and Whoosh! The whole fucking space around me just gave way like it'd been hit by a hurricane. I was on the ground and all these girls and boys were around me. Thank God they didn't flop in on top of me or I could easily have been injured or worse. It turned out not too bad, all things considered. I acted the little bully which meant I was able to foist myself back up onto my feet. There was now a large space containing seventy or so people who were lying horizontal on the floor . . . People too freaked and dumb to help one another. They were all like headless chickens, and it was difficult all round. Some really good guys – it was all guys – were holding the crowd back off of us and roaring at the people behind them to back off. They all finally got back up off the ground and the night went on. I didn't manage to really shift from my position for the rest of the set. I was stuck in the Bermuda Triangle. There were two more crowd rushes, neither quite as severe as the one that floored me. Every time the rush came I kind of gasped for air like I was about to drown. That was exactly what I felt like. Like I was about to be covered in water and drown."

It is a good idea to avoid entirely these indoor arena gigs. They're dangerous and unsatisfying; if you enter into an arena gig you should either stay at the back or go to the very front. If your band is a raucous guitar outfit you're literally taking your life in your own hands by burrowing out into the front centre of the crowd. The only advice for those who end up caught in a surge is to hold their ground and, if they can, organise every-body around them to do the same. Nothing is going to block a surge other than people standing their ground, no matter how improbable it seems that this strategy will have any effect. Keep both feet on the ground, don't freak out, and there is a good chance that those feet will stay on the ground.

Those interested in their clothes are advised to leave their best gear at home before moshing. Young boys will tend to ignore this rule, knowing that they'll be meeting their peers in the pit and that this is a unique chance to show off their new threads. This is fine for them. They can afford to be careless since most of the time their parents are paying for those expensive rags anyway. You need a strong pair of boots both to keep yourself firmly on the ground and to protect your feet. The same boys who like dressing up should avoid wearing long chains hanging from their belts or leather garments with spikes sticking out of them.

Rucksacks are totally unacceptable pit accessories. Girls are more guilty in the rucksack department, and skatekids in general regard rucksacks as being vital to their appearance. It doesn't matter that they're only in town for the night or that they have to crash on somebody's floor or that the rucksack contains their toothbrushes, Walkmans, and contraceptives. A rucksack takes up as much space as a human, and it converts a thin nimble kid into a bulky lump getting in the way of every-body, causing chains, belts, spikes, etc. to get caught up in the rucksack's various tassels and sashes.

If you see somebody wearing chains or spikes about to crowd surf, you should tell them to do something about the metal before they go up. It is one of the most consistent com-plaints you hear from those who get mild abrasions in the pit.

"One night at Slayer this guy crawled over me. He was being a careful enough dude but he had on this ancient battered black leather jacket which was covered in studs and spikes. As he slith-ered over me one of the spikes cut a gash in my head about two inches long. When I first felt the penetration of the spike I pulled at his hair, I shouted at him, I punched him in the balls. He thought I was just moshing with him and grinned at me like we were having a pleasant time together. He just didn't know. By the time the blood was flowing down my face he was gone. I'm lucky

it was my skull and not my eye or something. It looked worse than it was. I had to shave off all my hair to treat the wound but that was cool. I kept my head shaved for a year after that."

Don't bother standing alongside a big guy who seems friendly and capable. He'll probably help out up to a certain point but he'll be preoccupied with looking after Number One. I've been that big guy in many pits and, while its nice to help folks out for a while, you soon get weary of the remorseless requests for assistance from those who should have been better briefed on what to expect. It is cool to help people get up above the crowd to surf, but you get sick of heaving people up all the time. Also, it is naive to assume that the big guy is going to play Daddy for an hour. The big guy is as likely as not to take a negative view of your predicament, whatever that may be.

The final advice on the pit is somewhat controversial. If you're a girl, and you don't have experience in athletics or martial arts, and you're not a big strong boned girl, and you're not entirely au fait with what happens in the pit, you're probably well advised to consider giving the thrill a miss. A lot of the people who come out the worst from their pit experiences are women. Women can have a rough time out there. The unique solution is to go into the pit with your boyfriend and get him to protect you. If girls resort to this strategy they're flying in the face of pit theory, and they're missing out entirely on the thrills and spills.

Helen Kaye, who regards herself as a feminist, has a jaundiced view of women who survive in the pit by getting their men to protect them.

"You sometimes see girls in the pit with their boyfriends. The boyfriends have wrapped themselves entirely around the girls to protect them. There is nothing more craven looking or sick-inducing than this humiliating sight. It's kind of simian, stone

age. These 'sweet' little girls with their sweet Little Old Me smiles . . . with these huge orangutans standing behind them with their big protective hairy male arms wrapped firmly around their women. They stick together and kind of butt their way through the pit, the male in his element as a hunter-gatherer, glaring angrily at any guy who accidentally bumps into his bitch or, worse still, has a quick look at her.

"I have complete contempt for those women. What they're doing is so fucking sexist that its unbelievable. One of the feminist points you might make in favour of the pit, a kid of riot grrrl punk argument, might be that the woman who can stand alone in there, not breaking down crying because she's essentially a wuss, has achieved something for herself as a woman. Whereas those fools being protected by their men are insisting on long forgotten privileges to do with being a woman. Half the fucking point of going into the pit is to be on your own, to reject the conventional society."

Teenage Rampage

I first met Henry, Dusty and Ray at an early One Minute Silence gig. It was still One Minute Silence-against-the-world at that stage. Their fans were doggedly determined to follow them. It would be more accurate to say that we stumbled all over each other during a period of one hour when I helped Henry and Dusty hoist themselves up so that they could surf the crowd. By the end of the night the vibe between us was like we'd been lifelong friends though we'd never set eyes on each other until that very evening.

I never saw Ray again although he played an important part in Dusty and Henry's lives. I saw Dusty and Henry together about four times after that at One Minute Silence and at other metal bands with a danceable crossover aspect. After that Dusty kind of disappeared out of the picture – he had other problems. Henry I got to know very well and he was one of the people who marked my cards as I made my way through the layers under the surface of the pit. He showed up at one kind of gig and one kind only. His bands were never the mechanical metal-by-numbers cynics, they were always connected in on the beat. He liked industrial deviants like Revolting Cocks, distorted techno acts like Atari Teenage Riot and, at that time, he went to see One Minute Silence every time they played.

Dressed elegantly from head to toe in black leather he looked about 17. I think he was 20 when I met him. One of the first things I told him was that he still looked like a teenager. "I take that as a compliment," was his response. I can't remember who we were seeing that night. It was Rancid or The Deftones or Atari Teenage Riot.

When you go to the pit all the time the bands tend to drift into one another. Even with righteous bands for whom you have great affection, strong identities tend to drift out of focus. You remember a good night out not because of the band or its music, not even because of brief adventures and so-called crises in the pit. When you're moshing you remember a gig by the conversations you have with friends you meet there or friendly strangers who come up to you after the encores, thanking you for helping them out of whatever trouble they got into in the melee. They'll regale you with tedious war stories you've heard a thousand times before (for they are adolescents) or talk spontaneously about intimate aspects of their lives. What they think of their fathers – usually not a whole lot. How girls are strange – but well worth it. How they feel in the pit when paying homage to a band. How they'd love to get laid right there on the spot. Guy's stuff.

Henry lives alone in a two-up-two-down terraced redbrick owned by a father who seems to be a figure of mystery to him. Henry grew up in the English seaside town of Margate with his divorced mother and sister. The mother is a probation officer and the sister is doing postgraduate studies in New York.

Sometimes it seems like he's indifferent to his parents but sometimes he lets little things slip that make you think he has some warm feelings for his mother. He obviously respects his sister for her academic attainments. He finds it funny that his mother holds down a position within the state justice system. Henry himself is right out there on the social fringe, supportive of the Columbine High killers, interested in anything that really fucks up society. He says he totally relates to the Columbine killers.

"I despised the jocks and the macho clowns who went to school with me. They were so fucking stupid that I just wanted to kill them right then. I was living about 50 miles away from Columbine when the shooting happened so of course there was nothing else on the TV for weeks. I don't mean that I really think that it was good that they murdered those kids. But I certainly sympathise with the ones who did the shooting. I was laughing when it was all being reported on the TV and people were glaring at me, tut tutting, going on about the poor parents. I know what they mean but somebody had to do it."

His relationship with his father is strange. His folks' marriage broke up when Henry was seven and, while the family stayed on in the family home in Margate, the father moved into London where he did extremely well.

"I don't know what he does for a living. Maybe he does something in television. But I know he has loads of money. He lives with his girlfriend in Chelsea and he owns my house, and another house around the corner."

Henry talks continually about moving uptown, away from Canning Town, the rough East End district where, not long after I met him, a local gangster leader was assassinated in the pub right across from his home. He could surely afford to move away – he makes good money as a lighting man, working mainly on rock and theatrical gigs.

The real reason he stays in the East End is that he is locked into a social world of working guys and their young-mother girlfriends. Ecstasy, speed, and acid are weekend norms for a concrete jungle that Henry, as much an outsider there as anywhere else, finds amusing and intriguing. I think one of the reasons he liked hanging out with me was because we got to explore the many louche underbellies of Soho together. Compared with the drug killings and casual ruthlessness of the East End, the high jinks you see in Soho – mainly to do with money, sex, and where those two universes collide – seemed rather innocent or harmless. But it was a whole new universe to Henry.

When Henry first met Dusty, Dusty's best pal was Ray, whom I'd met briefly at One Minute Silence. Ray and Dusty hung around together at school in Canning Town. Henry was seventeen, Ray was around the same age, and Dusty was sixteen when they all hooked up. Dusty had been hanging out on the "wrong side of Canning Town" and his mother was worried about how he was going to turn out. When Henry arrived in town from Margate Dusty's mother was relieved when it looked like the two of them would become friends. Dusty's mother was not to know that what brought them together was the agit-rock of Rage Against The Machine and the angsty anthems of Nirvana. Dusty told Henry about Rage Against The Machine, Henry told him about Nirvana, they eventually dragged one another into the mosh pit.

Henry has clear memories of how the process of becoming a mosher began for him.

"It started in Margate. It was around '95. I was into Guns'n Roses. They seemed to be a commercial band and they were good. Just before I left school I started hanging around with a new bunch of people. A couple of them were into Nirvana. We used to go night fishing and there was one guy who brought down a tape to play. One side was Nirvana, the other side the Red Hot Chili Peppers. It was just music like anything else you might hear on the radio at first but I really got to like it. We didn't have any money so we couldn't buy any more music. So it was just one tape. Nirvana and the Peppers played over and over and over again all night. I got to know their songs by name. Who the artists were. I started buying their albums when I could. When I was about 15 I had one Iron Maiden album, a couple by Nirvana, a Chili Peppers album, and two by Gun'n Roses."

Those were the albums that Henry brought with him when he left his mother in Margate and moved up to his father's spare house in Canning Town. He soon met up with Dusty – he was working with Dusty's older brother – who was well into Rage Against The Machine but who hated the old school metal acts like Iron Maiden and Guns'n Roses.

> *"Dusty introduced me to Rage Against The Machine which I really liked. Their music just totally flowed. I don't know what album we were listening to. I think it must have been the first album and a couple of singles from the second one. Again, it was on a tape. Dusty had them on a cassette. I ended up buying a couple of Rage Against The Machine albums because I always had more money than Dusty. I was working a bit more than he was, and he would spend anything he had on drugs. So when we hung out together he had the dope and the cigarettes while I always had the record collection. I guess that was a good combination. He didn't mind sharing and I didn't mind sharing myself. I had this house belonging to my Dad to myself, so Dusty liked to hang out there. It was almost like an adult environment for a couple of reckless kids."*

Henry had smoked some hash before coming to London, and Dusty had been doing the same thing before they met up. Dusty's brother was a weekend cocaine user.

> *"One Monday morning he had some left over from the weekend so he introduced me to that at work. He offered me a line which gave me a little hit, nothing special. I think that's what it's like with cocaine at first. I ended up buying a gram that weekend. Dusty came over and he had a bit with me but he wasn't really interested. I didn't want to buy any more after that because it was just worthless. But then as more and more people around me had it I shared a line here and there so I got to appreciate it a bit more. So me and Dusty and Ray started doing cocaine. A lot!"*

104

Dusty was entirely reliant on dope to keep him on an even keel. He always had to have it and was violent and uptight like a bear with a sore head when he couldn't find any. He'd always make it his business to score. He'd sell personal stuff to get cash if he had to. In any case his brother-in-law was a dealer so he was always able to get some. "Dusty may be funny," Henry giggles, "but he did share his drugs when he had them."

When Dusty got his first job going around in a van making deliveries he seemed to straighten out and act responsibly. He was spending a little money on hash but he was also saving, displaying a side of himself that nobody'd ever seen before. He managed to put £1,000 into the bank and point blank refused to touch it. "He would always have some little bit to save away each week," Henry remembers, "no matter how much drugs he bought. He wouldn't want to spend £10 going out at the weekend. Then, when he met his first girlfriend he began to spend more and more on cocaine. She kind of corrupted him into spending his money. He began to change from then on. Now whenever he gets his hands on £10 he has to go and spend it on something."

COCAINE YOUTH SPARED PRISON went the headline in the local Canning Town rag about three weeks after I first met Dusty. He was walking down Barking Street in Canning Town, where the cops are always stopping and searching white youths like Dusty dressed from head to toe in white Adidas gear that fell off the back of a lorry. He had a packet of cigarettes with a foil of cocaine hidden within. The cops pulled up alongside him so he threw the box on the ground. A cop asked him a few questions and then picked up the cigarette box. They asked him if it was his and he denied it. "What? With the cigarettes in it? We don't believe you," one of them said.

They searched the box and didn't find anything. "Are you sure its not yours?" they asked. "Maybe it is mine," he said stupidly. They handed him the box and then the cop who was dealing with Dusty suggested to the other cop that he have a look inside the box. The cocaine was found. When they asked Dusty if he owned it he kind of shrugged and mumbled, "Yeah."

"He couldn't believe it when it appeared in the papers," Henry laughed. "He said they must have a journalist in the court all the time taking notes. His mother went mad when she saw it. His mum is a very nice person who'd never do drugs or anything, a very honest woman. The older brother, except for the cocaine at the weekends at that time, is a very good guy. He is a driver but he got fired because he was stealing shoes – just perks of the job. Apart from doing a little pilfering here and there he is very responsible. Now he works for the Royal Mail. He's not corrupt at all. Dusty's eldest sister had been around the block a few times with heroin and crack."

Shortly after I met the three guys at One Minute Silence, their friendship was rent apart by sexual intrigue.

Before Henry moved to Canning Town Dusty and Ray had been inseparable. Then they kind of drifted apart. By the time I met up with the three of them, Dusty was doing so much crack that Henry was giving him a wide berth. So Dusty started hanging around in Ray's place where Ray lived with his life-long girlfriend Corrina and the kid she'd had with Ray. Dusty'd play his Deftones and Slipknot records before crashing out in their spare bedroom.

One afternoon while Ray was out working Dusty was listening to music and smoking dope in the sitting room with Corrina. He said to her that he quite liked her, she said she felt the same way about him. Soon they were kissing and an affair commenced. Dusty and Corrina would have sex most afternoons while Ray was out at work.

Henry spent the next few weeks, every time he saw Dusty, strongly advising him to give it up. Ray was tough and had tough connections. The next time I ran into Henry there had been big developments. "Ray had *another* pal of his staying over one night last week." Henry grinned. "Dusty had gone to bed and so had Ray. Corrina decided she'd go downstairs to make herself a coffee and the new house guest, who was crashed out on the couch, started coming on to her. She told him to fuck off and went up to Dusty's room where they talked for a few hours before they both nodded off on his bed."

Early the following morning an irate Ray, when he didn't find his woman alongside him in bed, went into Dusty's room where he saw the two of them asleep on top of the bedcovers. "What the fuck is going on here?" he shouted. Dusty reacted smartly and told him that it was just that the guy downstairs had been chatting up Corrina so she came up to him all upset since he was still awake at the time. Then Corrina had just nodded off to sleep!

Ray went downstairs and gave his new guest a thorough trashing, pulling him onto the floor, kicking him around the place before dragging him out the door and dumping him on the front lawn. Then he went into the kitchen for breakfast and, half an hour later, left the house. When he saw his victim hadn't sufficiently recovered from his first beating to move on and was still lying prostrate on the lawn, he gave him another good kicking.

A few days later Dusty and Corrina were caught in action and Dusty went on the run with Corrina. Ray spent the next month roaming Canning Town with a gun looking for the runaways. Since then the dust has sort of settled, but Dusty is seeing a shrink every week to deal with his uncontrollable violent urges.

"Towards the end of the time that he was going moshing," Henry says, "Dusty was getting really violent in the pit. He'd say that sometimes he got so angry that he wanted to kill people. He was hooked on crack and couldn't hold a job down. He'd punch guys in the pit, he'd bite people. I didn't

107

like being in the pit with him. He liked to crowd surf himself but didn't have any give and take. He didn't play fair. When other people would surf over him he'd get really pissed off and punch them hard. In the end he stopped going to the gigs. I was the one who liked the gigs anyway. He didn't want to leave Canning Town or go out of town so much."

"In the early days it was always Dusty who was discovering the new bands. Slipknot and One Minute Silence. We were into Idlewild until they got a bit bigger and went shit. For me and Dusty the thing about One Minute Silence was that they were very loud, very fast, and very angry. That was more of an attraction to us than their political side. They were using fast drumbeats, fast guitars, and you could hear it in the singer's voice that he was raging about stuff. It was strange the way people would criticise them, saying that they were just a rip-off of Rage Against The Machine. If people didn't take a strong influence from other bands, there would be maybe six bands in the whole world so that'd be really boring. Anyway, with One Minute Silence, I felt that the singer also had a crazy sense of humour and I liked that.

"I started us off going to gigs a lot. We never even thought about going to gigs but my boss, who was a mechanic, was always going to gigs. Bob Dylan and Joe Cocker for instance. He encouraged me to try. The first thing me and Dusty and Ray went to was this kind of mellow indie band. Then we went to Idlewild at The Garage. Dusty had discovered them. I heard they were doing the gig so I bought the tickets. We went moshing there for the very first time. Not so much moshing as crowd surfing. I'd never seen anything like it in my whole life. I'd seen it in Wayne's World *and things but I thought it was just a joke in the movie. I didn't think people actually did it. But then we were there in The Garage at the front of the stage and, Oh My God! People were just getting up and coming over the top of us. My boss had always told me to go right to the front at gigs but he was*

thinking of Bob Dylan concerts! We were being crushed and Dusty was getting a bit pissed off with us being crushed all the time. But he was still liking it, with the band right in front of us and all.

"Then the climbing and the jumping went out of control. Next thing I knew I looked at the stage and there was Dusty up there alongside the band, and he stagedived into the pit. So I got up next and did the same thing. We had an amazing time. People were really friendly, bunking us up to crowd surf. We came out of there with a better feeling than drugs could ever give you. That started us going to gigs.

"Rancid at the Astoria was our first experience of a real mosh pit. It was pretty rough, I remember it being very open and we were more kind of running through the pit than getting involved with it. The pit was full of big guys who weren't being aggressive in any way. They were professional and friendly but we were very young and these guys were big experienced dudes with full dreadlocks and stuff. Closer to the front there were younger people, late teens, who were more bouncing and banging into one another. Further back where the real pit was the big guys had big spaces. They were making punching motions so if you happened to get in their way you connected. I would say that we were the youngest there.

"The best pits were the ones where people were about your own age and build. You got pushed around but it wasn't a hard push. You have to go into the pit with a certain attitude to moshing. When you're psyched up about a band anyway, and you get the chance to see them live, you get really psyched up beforehand about going into the pit. Like when we went to see Jesus Lizard. Dusty and me saw them as being very much tied up with the same scene which gave rise to Nirvana and, because the two of us had been so much into Nirvana, it was a big deal with us. We were so surprised that they were even playing, it was like a dream come true. If you're excited to see the band or to hear the

music, that can make a good pit. The funny thing is that quite a few people were there to see the support band The Pulkas. We got thrown out during their set and the bouncers let us in again ten minutes after Jesus Lizard came onstage. There were all these people who'd just come to see The Pulkas who were leaving, saying that Jesus Lizard were shit. I just couldn't believe my ears. That was one of the best pits I was ever in.

"One of the worst was possibly the Ozzfest. We were situated in a place where some people – older people who'd been into metal forever who didn't know too much about moshing – wanted to be at the front but didn't want to deal with all the crowd surfers. I was totally into it then but I've changed my mind about crowd surfing a bit since. I think it's kind of stupid or dangerous. Anyway, now I'm 22 so I think I'm a bit old for it. I used to really like to surf the pit.

In a big gig its weird. You float along and go up and down. Sometimes you go down so far that you're almost touching the ground but then people hoist you up again allowing you to cruise on towards the stage, up and down on a fantastic journey. Once I just got chucked into the air so that I almost did a somersault over hundreds of spectators before landing on a bunch of unexpecting people who can't have been too happy about me just landing on top of them out of the blue. They were punching me. Then there was this guy who just wanted to kick me in the head. Another time I fell down onto the ground and all the people around me started kicking me. When I got up again they all stared straight ahead pretending that nothing had happened. People do things in the pit at these big gigs that they'd never dream of doing in the real world. I think it's a mixture of the ano-nymity of the crowd and just the buzz.

When Ozzy Osbourne came on we made to leave since we weren't too interested in that kind of thing. Dusty in particular had no time for that old metal. We got on this coach heading back to London and there were these two girls we were talking to. One was in a neck brace and the other had a broken arm in a sling. They were right in the front for Coal Chamber. They said the crowd fell over and lots of people were getting kicked.

I prefer to mosh in clubs rather than at festivals. In a club, whether it's a 500-seater or a couple of thousand, it's still a club, and it has something of a family atmosphere in the pit. People will take note of you, spot you if you're in trouble. You're all there united to see one band. I've gone right down at gigs like that and there has been an immediate massive opening in the crowd. Everybody picks you up and pats you down. I think it feels great when people help you out in the pit. That's the best thing about it. It's almost like being at a rave, meeting new people and taking drugs with them.

One Minute Silence

Brian Yap Barry comes from Templemore, a small Irish town 40 miles from the small Irish town where I grew up. He moved from Ireland to the wild squats of London in the late Eighties, the drummer in a rock band. He recalls growing up in the small town Ireland of the Seventies and Eighties: "I was a pure fucking delinquent. The Templemore version of one. It was harmless. I was as naive as any other kid, but I never followed anybody."

Yap is a strange stage performer who seems to invoke the spirit of the diabolic every night he takes on the crowd. He is certainly exorcising something in himself through the writhing throbbing mosh pit. He learned something about the totemistic aspect of music back home in Ireland, where his folks are noted folk musicians. He told *Kerrang*: "One of my fondest memories is of a Sioux Native American Indian who did a traditional war dance in our sitting room. I was probably seven or eight, and it was quite surreal. He let his hair down – literally – down to his arse – and used my mum's bodhran. We were into cowboys and indians and we were always on the side of the indians so instinctively even back then we knew the Americans were full of shit politically."

He came to London with two friends who were in his band with him:

"I swear to God that we thought we would get off the boat and we would be famous. We could only see famous bands on Top Of The Pops, *we didn't know the underground existed. We ended up washing pots with all the illusions shattered. We woke up, we worked, we got by. I also remember the prejudice I faced. I was a carpenter for a while and I remember the police pulling me over in my van and throwing my tools on the road, checking the serial numbers and asking, 'Where have you stolen these from paddy?' 'They hit me and embarrassed me in front of British people who felt embarrassed too.'*

Right now Yap is the leader of One Minute Silence, the only London post-thrash posse with a hope in hell of competing out there in the arenas with the Slipknots and Limp Bizkits of this world.

The once-mighty English rock scene is more or less a thing of the past. London now has an industry-led band scene where wild excess – and the uncontrollable art that springs from that excess – is frowned upon. It is unlikely that London will ever again give rise to a Sid Vicious or a Brian Jones. Unless that troublesome troublemaker is Brian Barry. It is interesting to see his band, with a forthright social agenda strongly in place, doing well within the corporate world of Richard Branson's V2 label. One critic made the point that it is great that there is a London band avowedly anarchist but without the messy sartorials and predictable crusty image of bands like Chumbawamba.

When I spoke to Barry about rock'n'roll tradition he said: "Look! Rock'n'roll is dead. It was a great thing and nobody liked it better than me. I idolised those bands. And it was great that they achieved what they did. Heavy metal. Rolling Stones. Punk rock. The whole fucking thing is dead! So it doesn't matter what we say or what we do. The rules are off. The game is cancelled. End Of Story! We're all just out here on our own playing our songs and making the best of it."

An adolescent strike organiser at school, Barry is a whirlwind of intellectual, physical, and emotional activity. He struts the rehearsal room like he struts the stage, powerful and aggressive but in no way cocky or nasty. The multiculti world of his band – an English drummer, a young Italian punk guitarist, and a bass player from Gibraltar – reflects accurately the colourful cross pollination you encounter at their rough but principled pits. "Controlled violence" is how Yap, who moshes with the best of them when the hall is small enough so that it makes sense, describes the moshing at his gigs. This claim may be slightly disingenuous. Their pits are certainly the most harmonious I've been in, they have a first-rate pit crew, but violence definitely reacts off the turbulent music. I've seen real punches and real injuries at their gigs.

They're an outrageously powerful live act who achieve an impressive level of intelligent white noise while there is a white heat aspect to the moshing. I've seen them play and build themselves up from small club nights to 2,000 seaters. At most of those gigs the entire floor space was a pit. In the early days you had no business at a One Minute Silence gig unless you wanted to mosh. Their crowd included a lot of poor urban white kids who were kind of rough around the edges, maybe a 20 per cent ethnic crowd of Asians and Blacks, and the rest were the more sophisticated sort of punk and student aficionados who knew their onions when it came to edgy music.

They had a singer ranting and raving at them about any number of complex issues in a strong Tipperary brogue. If you thought, like most hardcore music fans in England did, that the rest of the world had all the sharp music, then One Minute Silence represented something special. Driven by a profoundly funky energy, they were danceable and women-friendly. Best of all they could think and give shape to those thoughts, a phenomenon all but extinct in London rock. So if you were 16 in London in '98 and you liked to think and mosh at the same time, they were the band for you.

They represented different things to different people. Very much in your face was their anti-racism. Barry is a great proponent of the argument that the Irish are the niggers of Europe: "You give me South Central LA and I'll give you South Central Tipperary. I'll give you 800 years of fucking oppression."

Like many others on the scene, the ghost of Kurt Cobain hovers over his head.

> *"I love Kurt Cobain, he was a genius. And he was a heroin addict, and that's very sad to have seen him fuck up on drugs. I think it's so bad to blow your fucking brains out. There's kids with no legs because of mines, there's kids starving and you can go on and on. And he had 20 million dollars and everything, and he stuck a fucking gun in his mouth. He was murdered some people would say, but well, that's speculation. I don't know. Maybe an alien killed him."*

Yap worked his deranged constituency like a politician, spending almost as much onstage time ranting to the delinquent mob in the pit as he did singing his songs. Solidarity and brotherhood in the pit were his main themes. The ranting appealed greatly to the new blank generation and to the pit derangement which went hand in hand with their lifestyle. Yap picked out the most loyal fans from the pit, dressed them up in uniform hip-hop gear, and appointed them the band's own security team operating from the pit. Their task was to make sure nothing too heavy happened.

He claimed that the structure of the live metal band and its fanatical followers was the perfect vehicle for the band's ideas:

> *"Definitely metal is the best music for delivering this form of message. I mean, everyone feels the same. I think anyone with a*

good heart and who is in any way compassionate about things like I am about the planet and racism, homelessness and so on. I have a platform to air my views and I think the best way to deliver them, an angriness if you like, is with metal music. And I think metal music is soul music, and the soul is about emotions. Like blues is about someone pissed off at love as an emotion. And anger is an emotion and so it's soul music. Like if you're angry and pissed off at something you just scream. And metal is aggressive music so it's the best medium I think for our delivery."

Sometimes it seemed that their show was a little too slick and rehearsed. But they were a real enough item to cut through that, they had a great hardcore mechanical rev about them. There was an out-of-control aspect of Barry as front man that delivered an inevitable nasty reality to the show. When I visited them in their East London rehearsal studio they were obviously in the middle of a gruelling rehearsal which saw them achieve an almost military precision. I was struck by their puritan commitment to the hard work involved in having the edge. Not so puritan, however, that the air didn't reek with the smell of marijuana.

There is an accusation that their message is mundane: *Racism is bad, shagging is good, all policemen are pigs.* Barry was unapologetic about encouraging moshers: "It's their stage. If there's 50,000 at a gig and 40,000 want to get onstage, get up . . . We've had gigs in London where my monitors have been wrecked within two minutes because people got onstage, and I was going 'Made my fucking night.' "

There was one spectacular melee at the Camden Palace: "We were trying to incite a riot. Come on down. Jump off the barriers and break your neck, y'know. And some people took offence to it. 'You want people to break their necks.' Course I don't want them to. Yeah I want to meet them in the pit and a mosh frenzy." He thinks that in the mosh pit you can see both the good and bad side of humans. Bassist Glen Diani, a dreadlocked lothario, said: "It is the only kind of music where you can bang each other and you help each other out. They're killing each other throughout the song and then between songs they're like best friends."

"I genuinely don't want to see people getting hurt," Yap insisted. "We had someone come up to us at a festival in Portugal. There was a mosh pit with 2,000 people. Kid came in, his lip was split open, and his head was all stitched up. He came up and was like, 'Man. I did that in your mosh pit,' and he was delighted. And he had his battle scars. We say 'Kill. Kill' but we don't mean that. Just wound each other! And then rub each other."

He was not one of those band leaders who plays with the heads of not fully formed adolescents. He ranted against a Slayer album cover:

> *"I hate the band Slayer for putting that image on their album sleeve. Kids are impressionable and I hated them for thinking slicing Slayer into your arm is cool. There could be a Slayer fan who died ten years ago who did it on his stomach and died because his parents weren't around and Slayer will never know that. A bunch of fucking morons if you ask me. If a One Minute Silence fan came to me with our logo carved into his arm I would give him the number for a shrink!"*

He has gone on stage with eighty three stitches in his body.

He said cutting himself was a cathartic experience. "The last time I did it I cut right through my T-shirt and sweatshirt into my body and was really pushing the blade in. I needed three stitches in my chest. I couldn't even pick up a blade now. I can't imagine doing it.

"I can't explain it," he said. "I can't comprehend being black you know? I can just read about it and listen but unless you're depressed you can't understand it. I actually remember cutting myself back in school, daring everyone to see who can do the biggest cut . . . I just think it took over, it went mad. Five fucking years . . . I'm a little more in control now, that's all it is, and sometimes I lose it."

It's this tough/fragile aspect of Yap which appealed to the kids. "I like Yap because he is obviously fucked up," said one boy I met all the time in the One Minute Silence pit. "Sometimes he looks like a samurai and sometimes he is well overweight. So you know he's human. And he talks such bullshit on stage. I think he's great."

Yap wore his heart on his sleeve, alive to the fact that we live in a nasty world:

> *"The trouble with the planet is this hippy dippy dovey flower power thing was nice, but it doesn't work. You can't fucking fight scum with flowers. If someone comes at you with a baseball bat and you turn the other cheek, you're in hospital on a drip for six months. I ain't turning the other cheek for nobody. I ain't attacking nobody. I'm not advocating violence."*

He denied, despite his confrontational style, that he was in any sense personally violent, or that the band incited violence:

> *"I've never hit anybody and I've never been in trouble with the law and I never intend to. People may think I'm a big intimidating frontman. I'm not. I'm an ordinary guy and I've a lot of fucking problems like everybody else. We may come across as a violent band, and we love the energy of the mosh pit, and we love people jumping around but we don't want them to kill each other. It's not fun. I may encourage people to come up and bite my face onstage, but I don't want any fucking bites y'know."*

"Teenagers are scapegoated along with single parents and drugs." Yap told *Kerrang*: "There's nothing wrong with promiscuity. There is a problem with rape and non-consensual sex but after that you do your own thing."

Two gigs in which the pit got out of hand and trashed the venue catapulted One Minute Silence out of the bars and into the halls. When they played at London's industry-friendly venue The Borderline the place got mashed. About two hundred junior teens, egged on by the band, went into turbo drive. After a while a small number of them started hanging from water pipes hinged onto the venue's ceiling. The pipes gave out and cracked pretty quickly. Endless gallons of water filled the floor and resulted in the entire crowd slipping and sliding chaotically as the band reached the peak of their set. As Yap told *Kerrang*: "At the Borderline show someone jumped on a water pipe and it burst. We loved it because it's rock'n'-roll. But we didn't plan it. When it came to the Garage show we'd sold out already. Everybody was waiting for a sequel. When we got onstage security were beating up fans. The next thing I knew the shit had hit the fan."

The shit – or rather the moshers – literally hit the fan at The Garage, one of a number of venues owned by the Mean Fiddler Organisation, who control a substantial chunk of the London small venue circuit, and the important Reading Festival, an obvious target for crowd pleasers like One Minute Silence. Egged on by Yap's transparent exhortations to them to "go crazy tonight", the small venue erupted. The security, well used to hardcore bands and pits, reacted negatively. A number of the band's most fanatical fans, including some of their pit crew, were thrown out in the first few minutes of the set. Outside the venue these kids, who were doing nothing more than moshing aggressively, were allegedly punched about by security.

Word of this reached Yap later in his set. He immediately stopped playing and told the pit to destroy The Garage. Kids attacked the condom and cigarette machines and tore a huge air-conditioning fan, which hung right over the pit, from the ceiling. They looted expensive microphones, and inflicted grim injuries on themselves. This frenzy of destruction was the result of an hour of steadily nastier moshing during which, as one kid put it to me, "It was really happening for me. I was out there in the middle of the mosh, about three hundred guys, and I was punching out, creating a free space for myself."

As a result of that particular night of passion One Minute Silence began to grow famous. Label boss Branson had only one thing to say when he heard about the chaos: "Was there enough media there?" There was tons of media present and, better still, hundreds of agitated adolescent mouths willing to generate invaluable word-of-mouth. The Mean Fiddler Organisation banned the band from all their venues and festivals. This was bad news for the boys; Reading would have been an obvious next platform for them. Within months One Minute Silence were selling out 1,000-seater venues beyond the reach of the Mean Fiddler.

Like his fans, Yap's favourite phrase is, "I don't give a fuck." He is smart and dark just like those fans, an interior man in an exterior business. After we'd smiled wryly and silently about that night in The Garage he went on to explain: "I don't give a fuck about the Mean Fiddler or Vince Power's fucking air con-ditioning. Those kids who come to see us in the mosh pit are the best kids in the world. I'd die for them. They'd die for me. The most important thing in the world for me is having these fans to play for."

Many guys in bands come out with this sort of guff and what they actually mean is that the most important thing in the world for them is that their fans should keep spending ever-increasing amounts of money on their gigs, merchandise, and CDs. Yap is scathing on the topic of American stadium rock bands, their affluence, and their cynical distance from their legions of rebel disciples. A One Minute Silence song attacks the reactionary nature – and the reactionary stance – of stadium rock, the song's chorus a mantra attacking the fraudulent onstage exhortations which are the meat and potatoes of some mosh pit bands:

Great to see ya.
Another day, another dollar.

One wonders how Yap will cope if he actually gets rich and famous – difficult to jump into the mosh pit when you're playing 5,000 seaters like Brixton Academy or outdoor festivals where there can sometimes be 30 feet between stage and pit. Difficult to chat with the fans from behind the tinted glass of a limousine.

Interested in the contradictions between rock glamour and the very real alienation which the fans experience, I asked Yap how he actually got to meet these people he claimed as his soul brothers. The question didn't throw him but it did stall the torrent of vague platitudes about what great people his fans were. He got very, plausibly, specific.

"Well . . . we employ people from the pit . . . and after a gig some guys would come backstage to chat with us . . . or meet us when we're loading the gear into the van afterwards. Some nights they'll have travelled all the way from London to see us three hundred miles away so I'd ask them how they intended getting home and the answer would be that they were going to hang around until the first train the following morning. So we'd load as many of them as we could into the back of the van and take them back to London."

Drummer Eddie Stratton, in an interview with *Anti Fascist Action* admitted that he "had been brainwashed by a very dangerous cult group called Scientology. I was a committed racist homophobic elitist. I blamed the poor for being poor." He now quotes Chomsky and the American Sociological Review in his interviews and is strongly committed to anarchism. He told *Anti Fascist Action*: "The story goes that because of our propensity towards self-destruction we clearly can't do without agents of order to stop us running around stealing, raping and killing everyone, so we have to have a bunch of very clever, scrupulously honest people in charge who are somehow so superior in that they conveniently don't share this flaw in human nature which we plebeians have."

Calm Like A Bomb –
Rage Against The Machine

Tom Morello used to point out that it made perfect sense for his band to campaign against clothing manufacturers who used sweatshop labour. He said that the demographic that bought those cool T-shirts was the same demographic that bought Rage Against The Machine albums. This off-the-cuff comment betrayed one of the contradictions at the heart of the band's great experiment. They preached fringe politics using mainstream music. It hardly came as a surprise that they attracted a mainstream crowd, the kind of people who were content to be happy slave consumerists buying Nike and other contentious garments.

The contradictions involved in Rage Against The Machine don't really concern the contrast between their far-left politics and their status as very rich rock stars. Every progressive popular band has to wrestle with that particular question, and it is usually resolved by slumping into contented middle-aged wealth. The actual contradiction is the conflict between their opposition to rock's elitist traditions and the fact that – like Pearl Jam – they practised their art at traditional rock stadium shows where they were heavy on the guitar. At those gigs they had an activist pit, there were loads of solid political flyers distributed, and a large cross-section of the crowd were the usual bozos you see anywhere.

Before Zack De La Rocha quit Rage Against The Machine he spoke of his anger at aspects of the Frankenstein he'd helped to create. "Personally I don't recognise the boundaries between music and political action," De La Rocha said. "But as an artist I can't sit around talking shit and collecting royalty cheques. This isn't something I see as a way to create change in my lifetime."

Son of a Chicano artist and a teacher mother, De La Rocha used his vastly successful band to promote a variety of political causes, and spent a lot of time in Mexico's Chiapas province working with the Zapatistas. He was one of the few artists to talk frankly about the contrast between his material wealth and the ideals he'd pursued since he was a teenage straight edge punk rocker.

His role as a big-shot rock star perturbed him. His band had helped forge the connection between punk and hip hop – a great experiment in its day – but the end result of that great experimentation was Limp Bizkit and the Woodstock riots. Seeing what happened at Woodstock was one of the many things which forced De La Rocha to go solo, investigating his penchant for hip hop and other dance disciplines. He despaired of what he saw happening at Woodstock. He spoke of "kids just dancing around in a way they saw in so many videos on MTV, beating each other up and tearing each other's hair out, doing this stupid little ritual." Guitarist Tom Morello was more sanguine about what they achieved live, saying that their audience was one of the more rabid and feverish around. He said it was like grabbing a live wire to step onstage with Rage Against The Machine.

Morello, a Harvard-educated Marxist, was quick to boast of their political achievements. Speaking to *Rock Sound* at the time when De La Rocha was considering his options, Morello waxed lyrical about their achievements.

"The platform that having a new Rage Against The Machine record gives us means we can really show people how to be a revolutionary rock band. We've had some success building bridges between our audience and the grass roots organisations that we endorse, but I think we can do a lot more. You see, there's a culture in America now where you blame young people; Woodstock, the Columbine massacre. And it's nothing new – each successive generation is blamed for society's ills. And now the music that kids listen to is demonised along with them. President Clinton made a hugely hypocritical statement after Columbine when he went on TV and said we must not use violence to settle our differences. Forty eight hours later a US Tomahawk missile blew up a bus of elderly women and children in Yugoslavia, and they also blew up a hospital. That's a war crime. So in America you scapegoat computer games and Marilyn Manson and ignore the rest. They're terrified for instance of the gun lobby so they blame everyone else."

Marxist or not, it looks like Morello took a more elitist view of his own power as a rock god than De La Rocha, who wrote all Rage Against The Machine's lyrics and half their music. Morello may have been disparaging De La Rocha's grass roots activism when he said: "We're not interested in preaching to just the converted. It's great to play abandoned squats full of anarchists but it's also great to be able to reach people with a revolutionary message." De La Rocha, for his part, was not entirely free of hubris. He too rated their achievements highly: "What makes it exceptional with us is the time period we came from – a greedy, greedy era. Rage happened in the face of critics who had abandoned the possibility of music to effect change. I think we proved they were wrong."

They endured their fair share of mosh pit problems. During a Seattle '96 show, a fourteen-year-old boy, Scott Stone, suffered a severe brain injury. Nobody saw exactly what happened, and it proved difficult to pin down exactly how he got injured. What was never in doubt were the devastating results of his injuries. Parts of his memory disappeared, he lost twenty points on his IQ ratings, and a court-appointed guardian recommended that he be declared mentally incompetent. "His rights will be limited to that of a minor," his attorney said. He would no longer make up his own mind about things like signing a contract or getting married.

There were lots of cases like that one. It was difficult for guys who were forever doing benefit concerts and giving away show fees to causes to square that stance with playing to the big crowds and shifting truckloads of CDs. I was once involved in a festival in Madrid where Rage were headlining the big outdoor festival stage. The promoter, a Spanish anarchist, told me that the entire Rage Against The Machine fee went straight to the Zapatistas. There were representatives of the Zapatistas at the festival.

Zack De La Rocha grew up in Long Beach during the Eighties listening to gangsta rap and hardcore punk. He joined two straight edge local bands, Hardstance and Inside Out, before hooking up with Morello in '91 to form Rage Against The Machine. The band name was borrowed from an Inside Out song of that title. Rage's first eponymous album came out in '92. Since then they've sold more than 10,000,000 albums.

It is perhaps ironic that a band which sought to break the theatrical conventions of the rock show relied, rather heavily, on the oldest of crowd response tricks to get things moving. Theirs was a very old-fashioned onstage style. De La Rocha regularly exhorted his crowd to join him in shouting out assertions of individuality such as "They say jump, you say how high" and "Fuck you. I don't want to be like you." It was legitimate for *Rolling Stone* to question, in '99, the extent to which Rage Against The Machine's activism was rubbing off on their crowd.

> *"How much of the band's political message sinks in with the fans? As they flipped the bird en masse to some invisible energy, were they really showing support for the band's stance on certain pet issues? Or were they expressing their contempt for more local authorities, like their parents, teachers, and bosses? The still more important question is whether it even matters how many members of the crowd are fledgling proselytisers. Regardless of their political savvy, the fans were, for barely an hour, united in their sense of alienation and discontentment."*

Some fans, mind you, were savvy enough to make their own points about the politics on offer. When a seventeen-year-old boy with a heart condition died of a heart attack in their pit after a '97 show in Indiana, one fan of the band wrote a letter to his local paper which pointed out the very contradictions which subsequently caused De La Rocha to quit the band: "They had this big speech about don't go to Wal-Mart because of censorship. What about dying? That's censorship. You should be able to go and listen to music and not be in fear for your life."

Tom Morello made a legitimate defence of their populist style when he pointed out that not all their shows took place in front of well-fed mosher kids in the West.

> *"We just got back from playing a show in Mexico City, which was just off the hook as far as being where the music meets the politics. The show was opened by a speech from Zapatista leader Subcomandante Marcos, via videotape, in part about the situation there in Mexico, in part about Rage Against The Machine and their audience. And it was really incredible. And as we were walking offstage, Zack said to me, 'When people raise the finger and say, "Fuck off. I won't do what you tell me!" it resonates in a different way when you're facing some of the things they're facing here, as opposed to what they're facing in maybe Peoria, Illinois.' But it's a healthy sentiment in Peoria, too."*

Obviously as they walked offstage Rage Against The Machine had conversations which differed greatly from the normal banter you get out of bands as they stride triumphantly towards the backstage after the encores.

Many people you meet at hip gigs used to be into Rage Against The Machine, and many of them still hold a torch for them, as you do for the first bands you were ever into. Their fans have spread out into the entire range of scenes. Many have gone on to hip hop, and a lot into more radical rock styles. An Atari Teenage Riot fan, after talking to me about collaborations between the two bands, recalled when she was sixteen and into Rage Against The Machine.

> *"I somehow expected it to be more radical the first time I saw them, which must have been early in '99. I expected there to be something more to them than the rap-rock formula. In fact there was hardly even a rap aspect to that show, and I was a little bit disappointed. It seemed boring and in many ways the band seemed bored too. I was never surprised that they split because what I was seeing onstage contradicted everything that Zack, particularly, claims to stand for. Then about four months later I saw them at Reading Festival and it was a whole other story. They're not the only band from that time who were way better with the vast crowd than they were in a hall. Their own personal chemistry seemed to grow as they fed off the crowd — it was, like, a 20,000 people mosh pit. Zack didn't say all that much at Reading, but you could just sense that he was much more focused on his gig. It was like seeing two different bands."*

Mate Feed Kill Repeat – Slipknot

On a cold night in March 2000 I headed for the Brixton Academy to catch Slipknot, who'd clawed their way to the top on the back of their mosh pit outrages, over the injured bodies of thousands of fans all over the world. They'd been under siege from MASK (Mothers Against Slipknot) who'd started riots at their US concerts claiming that Slipknot were telling their sons and daughters to make a slipknot, tie it to a rafter, then to just put their necks into the noose and jump. Vocalist Corey said: "I swear to God this is so much fucking bullshit. I can't believe these bitch mothers."

A product of Des Moines, Iowa, Slipknot are the ultimate small town band. According to their drummer Shawn they were all raised pretty well but they were raised in an environment where you had to develop your own sense of individuality. "I had 16,000 imaginary friends," Shawn says. "I had my own fucking army. Where we came from you don't really have an outlet to let go. That's why we stuck with this for ten years." They like a reactive crowd and find it difficult to deliver their best without a mosh pit. One of them said he really fed off the crowd, that when the crowd was just standing still and staring at them he wanted to throw his guitar down and start smacking people.

They adopt an almost straight edge attitude to drugs and debauched behaviour. Any member who steps out of line is in danger of being fired out of the band. At the end of one typical period of extended '01 touring, they had to abandon the tour when one member became "sick". There were subsequent alleged arguments within the band over which they pulled a veil of secrecy. They talked like they were a football team rather than a rock'n'roll band. They spoke of "practices" rather than rehearsals. Percussionist Chris said they were maintaining "an excellent practice schedule for the last three years. Everybody's on time, everybody's always there, and we always practise as a unit."

In January 2000 an Oklahoma City show had ended with complete riot conditions in effect. The promoter had oversold the gig. Fans were scanned by search-beams from helicopters and dragged away in handcuffs by local police. Then Slipknot refused to perform when they heard that some of their kids had been thrown out and the unrest erupted inside the venue.

Even the band members themselves grew weary of the mayhem. Chris said that the one thing he didn't like about their shows was the paranoia surrounding "who will come on stage and tackle the clown next, because it's starting to go to a new level. I used to tell people 'come and kill the clown' and now it's actually happening."

The last time they'd played London, December '99, their twenty-one-year-old DJ Sid threw himself from the thirty five feet balcony of the London Astoria into the mosh pit down below. He later did it again, this time falling backwards into the crowd.

Their album *Slipknot* was the fastest selling metal debut in the history of the American Soundscan chart. Producer Ross Robinson implied that their attitude to studio work was similar to the spirit of their live shows. It sounds like the album was recorded in a private mosh pit atmosphere. "It was total chaos," Robinson remembered. "The band were slamming, just like at a show. They were all three feet in the air with shit getting slammed and hit, and drums getting thrown at the wall."

While Marilyn Manson and Limp Bizkit can be seen as cynical corporate exercises in unit-shifting, there is a definite sense that Slipknot, like One Minute Silence, are caught up in a very real way in the world they scream and rant about. In their small town nobody gave a shit about them until they began to attract a crowd. Whether there is a cynicism about their stance or not, there can be no doubt but that – at the very least – they're stranded in the middle of a Frankenstein of their own making.

A month after their Brixton show *www.clevescene.com* reviewed their gig in Cleveland, talking about "metal-loving meatheads, a legion of half-naked Gothic mall girls", before going on to denounce their tunes as "A pocketful of third-rate metal licks and enough f-words to make Andrew Dice Clay look like Mary Poppins . . . the musical equivalent of a low budget slasher movie."

A few days before the Brixton gig, at Wolverhampton's Civic Hall DJ Sid repeated his Astoria trick of the year before. He dived thirty feet from the balcony into the mosh pit, giving head and spinal injuries to the teenage girl he landed on. She subsequently refused to press charges, saying that it was the best gig she'd ever been at. The *Guardian* gave substantial news coverage to efforts to have the tour cancelled, and disparagingly mentioned the lower middle class, and moronic, nature of the band's followers. There was talk of "teenage sweat and misguided testosterone".

Whereas Marilyn Manson represents a controlled freakery, a middle-of-the-road MTV and Net-friendly shocker given to covering Eurythmics songs, there is no doubt but that Slipknot have emerged from a very real stew of disillusionment, disenfranchisement and misanthropy. They're always at pains to mention their provincial roots. They're from the exact same

background as the Trenchcoat Mafia of anti-jock geeks responsible for the Columbine High slaughter. They appeal to a community working in shitty going-nowhere jobs, or to those
imprisoned in school – imprisoned because the only future
looming up in front of them is one of dead-end jobs on
dead-end streets.

I had an appointment to interview Slipknot founder and
main drummer Joey Jordison. I got to the back entrance of the
Academy, walking through an atmosphere of unbelievable
excitement. The feeling I got from the thousands of Slipknot
fans, who were both queuing to get in and milling about to no
good purpose, was that their excitement derived from something other than looking forward to seeing their favourite
band. Those kids had the complete look of outsiders about
them.

Although Slipknot have railed against the notion that they
attract fat and ugly kids, an offensive attitude in itself, there is
some truth in the accusation. There were very few babes or
pretty boys in this throng. They all seemed to be too thin, too
tall, obese, spotty, or just plain introverted. The girls tended to
be of the fat and shrill variety that you usually come across at
goth or traditional metal shows. The girls displayed definite
mother hen symptoms, remorselessly gathering their pals
around them, capable ladies geared up to a high level of
anxiety. They were, all in all, a friendly crowd and, it must be
said, nice people. Very definitely in from the suburbs and the
satellite towns.

A Beatlemania-style atmosphere characterised the Stage
Door. I had to be dragged through about 70 schoolkids who'd
won phone-in competitions. They were getting to meet the
band backstage.

While waiting in the dressing room for Joey to arrive I
heard, loud and proud, the strong Irish accent of One Minute
Silence's Yap out in the corridor. They were supporting

Slipknot, a good break for them. Soon I was joined by Joey, a good-looking short little guy who was hyper for the gig ahead. Part of the Slipknot spiel is that their individual masks reflect something about their personalities. Joey's mask, a white as porcelain Japanese Noh-style piece, was very soothing and attractive, whereas all the other masks are frightening and monstrous. He looked exactly like a lot of the tough little runts you come across in their pit. About five foot tall, he looked like he could take care of himself. When he talked there was structure to what he had to say.

He agreed that one of the things the band members shared in common with their audience was a sort of decent lower-middle-class background. He said their crowd was "totally labour-like kids. When I got a part-time job as a kid I got a $100 cheque every other week and it went right into music. I didn't save it for nothing. Blew it right away. If I had fuckin' ten bucks and I could buy a CD or food I bought a CD."

Joey was civilised and smart. He gave good copy, you didn't feel that what he was saying to you was a talking press release. He plugged the band like fuck but I think he was actually proud of what they'd done. He was very much small-town and proud of it. The band's going-nowhere background was some-thing they shared in common with a lot of the bands who were coming on strong right then: "Those kids are so gung ho on what we do. We speak directly to them. Not above them. Not below them. In their language, heart to heart. They take that and they wear it on their sleeve."

His assessment of various different moshing scenes was shrewd. He reckoned that in America moshers are not up to much. "Half of them are jumping," he said, "half of them are pitting, half of them are standing like idiots, half are eating. Some are drinking. Half the time they don't know what they're fucking doing."

He felt that in Japan and Australia the fans got much more

worked up and intense about it all because they didn't get to see so many bands. "Over there they'll all be jumping like a motherfucker, a lot of the shows in Europe are like that too. Way more coalesced into one ball of energy."

He had a low opinion of those wretches who cowered safely at the back of the arena. "The people at the back can fuck off," he spat out. "They're name droppers. You didn't see them queuing outside the record store at 10 a.m. the day our new album came out. When I watch bands – I went to the SnoCore tour which featured System Of A Down, Mr Bungle, Incubus. I had backstage passes. Fuck that. I'm watching from out front. That's the way a band is playing – out to *that*. They're putting energy out that way, and that's the way it's being received."

They make it their business to get to meet the sometimes odd and dysfunctional looking kids who follow them. Joey says he knows personally the core fans in the various cities who are the major players in the Slipknot pits: "I know all those guys to speak with one on one, not even necessarily about the band but about life in general. 'How're you doing?' and 'Thanks for coming.' 'How's the kids?' or 'What d'you do for a job?' You got to meet them one on one. That's why we have so many fans. We'll stand out in the rain for hours after the show to make sure that shit is signed."

He refused to denounce the Trenchcoat Mafia-style lyrics of Slipknot, while acknowledging that their campaign to infect the youth with their ideas would undoubtedly end grimly: "I'm pretty much sure that soon someone's going to have a really bad accident like the Columbine thing. It's eventually going to come to us. Shit like that." He told a journalist: "When the time comes to fight, then sure we'll fight. Then we'll fuckin' get naked. We'll take it one step further. We'll come naked and bleeding. We'll come plain dying."

In interviews Joey was unapologetic about what happens to victims of the pit, including the Wolverhampton girl with the spinal injuries. None of it, he assured, was supposed to happen. "Our fans know that we're really fucked up about it when this sort of stuff goes down. But it hits the people it's supposed to hit. They're almost like chosen." The way he saw it, their burgeoning popularity was payback time for middle America. "All of us were so used to having the middle finger thrown at us that when we finally threw it back, we did it with ten times the venom."

I made my way into the hall. One Minute Silence hit the stage unannounced, to the colossal surprise of the crowd. They wallowed in a noisy triumph, their power increasing as they came to terms with a raucous and tough looking pit which extended all the way to the back of the crowd. Difficult to see how Slipknot, for all their legendary assault skills, could top this. It seemed that a more muscle-bound male crew dominated the pit during the One Minute Silence set. The more typical Slipknot kids made their mischief a little further back.

Whereas Marilyn Manson toys with a dubious and opportunist bisexuality, there is about Slipknot and their fans a very bleak sense that, while heterosexuality is their option, they don't think much of it. Their heterosexual role models are often divorced parents and dysfunctional families. They've reached an age when most kids are having the joys of sex – or at least fantasising about it. For some of the Slipknot kids sex is the beginning of a soulless repetitive cycle of breeding and dying. One boy near me, about 14, wore a T-shirt which said "This is your world in which we live and we will grow to hate you."

The initial frenzy caused by Slipknot making their noise subsided. There was much screaming of "fuck" from behind the sex fetish masks that the band wore. They called on the crowd to go for it but calls to war were surplus to requirements in a war zone. A lot of people were having fun but a lot of passive violence was happening while a lot of stupid business was going on. The music amounted to little more than raw rhythm so everything was based on the relationship between band and pit. The programmed techno hip-hop nu-metal was fuelled by three drummers. You were getting hit – standing right there in front of huge columns of speakers – by a powerful, if mindless, rhythmic assault. Joey was right when, earlier, he'd described that sound as being "the sound of the triangle, the pyramid. The power of the guitar. Cerebral. Primal. All that."

The gawkers at the very back had a field day. It was a chance for the grown-ups to see two infamous phenomena, this band and their audience. Because of the outrage factor, more middle-aged people had heard of Slipknot and Marilyn Manson than possibly had heard of any wave of bands since The Beatles and The Stones. Many adults, lots of them media people, were in the Academy to see this manifestation of what Marilyn Manson calls *disposable teens*. The nobodies who want to be somebodies when they die.

The mosh pit works the best when you have a decent guitar-led rock band like Rancid or Soulfly. A strange self-discipline takes over and people punch each other out, crowd surf, indulge in celebratory circle moshes, with no problems and limited injuries. The moshing during One Minute Silence was powerfully disciplined, guided by mature self-appointed lieu-tenants, exciting to watch or participate in. There was a serious level of uproar fuelled by remorseless beats, sex energy, and that indefinable turn-on that derives from violence.

Bands reliant on alternative musical disciplines, like Slip-knot, don't always enjoy so agreeable a pit. Their music is not what was once called rock music. That is more or less dead. So instead of rising up to some profound exhortation of the dia-bolic spirit of freedom like The Rolling Stones or Iggy Pop in their respective primes, Slipknot's set went round in circles. Very toe-tapping, very dance-inducing, very powerful, much the same effect as listening to techno. Soon the pit was declining into a chaotic frenzy where the spirit of live-and-let-live gave way to a nastier, harder edge. Huge older guys, full of Dutch courage, elbowed and punched the lighter kids out of the way. Fights were breaking out. Italian anarchists were screaming at ageing American punks. Selfish crowd surfing was happening at a fierce rate, and surfers were persistently disappearing into the crowd.

The danger with crowd surfing lies in the fact that the surfers are coming at you from behind. Your attention is focused on the musicians onstage or on the rage going on right in front of you. You're trying to keep both feet firmly on the ground, you spend a lot of time crushed like a sardine balancing yourself on one foot or attempting to maintain your composure with both feet off the ground. You're incapable of controlling your own movements and actions. The five hundred people in front of you look like they're about to collapse on top of you so you're leaning backwards at a forty-five degree angle trying to stay in the vertical while the dude in front of you is trying to do the same thing. And the crowd surfers keep coming from behind like incoming troops wriggling across the ground.

A black girl close to me wearing a black Soulfly T-shirt was really getting off on the band. A crowd surfer having difficulty staying afloat stretched out his left hand for support. Involuntarily he clutched the girl's right breast rather fiercely. When he saw what he was doing he instantly removed his hand. For a minute the girl didn't react at all. Then, her innocent assailant long gone, she started screaming and crying. She totally freaked out and had to be helped out of the pit, unsure and confused.

Black girls in the mosh pit are non-existent. In Europe black guys are thin on the ground. The issues of women and Blacks in the mosh pit are much discussed in moshing-related websites. It has long been the case that, while white kids love black music, black kids are not terribly interested in the musical fare we have on offer. This largely explains the absence of large numbers of ethnic kids in some pits. Anti-racism, preached by the likes of Rage Against The Machine and Soulfly, is a major bonding principle of the pit and one of the most attractive characteristics of the people you meet there. The problem of women in the pit is a whole other issue connected with topics like promiscuity, sexual harassment, and the sometimes stupid behaviour of girls either unfamiliar with the conventions of the pit or, to put it simply, way out of their league.

But the girls tend to be light (although the more seasoned female mosh pit veterans can be big girls) and the most dangerous crowd surfer is the fat boy who thinks he has a Peter Pan-like physique and a similarly fairy-ish ability to fly through the air. When the fat boys have it in mind to crowd surf, their pals assist them in getting up above the crowd and, using every ounce of lard at their disposal, they propel them-selves up into the air and across the crowd.

Being big lads they don't tend to fly very far. And when they land they land on you or on somebody just like you. The most serious injuries and near-catastrophes I've encountered in the mosh pit all derive from inexperienced crowd surfers and stage-divers. This happened to me about five minutes after Slipknot arrived. A big teenager who must have weighed at least three hundred pounds landed directly on my head. For one second I thought I was going to collapse completely. My legs buckled, there were stars in my eyes, and my neck felt dis-tinctly crushed. Nothing serious came of it but I was stunned. The confusion in which I made my way through the pit was responsible for my next, much more serious, mishap.

The last thing anyone wants to happen in the pit happened. Like fatal tidal waves, crowd surges came upon me when I was totally off guard. Suddenly, just like a wave, I saw people in front of me tumbling to the ground like a house of cards. The visual form of this type of collapse is similar to the earth subsiding in an earthquake. There was a black hole full of writhing and struggling bodies, stricken on the ground, in mortal danger from the other people tumbling in on top of them. Like the people behind me, I had seconds to react to this development. The only option was to vigorously, selfishly, retreat backwards. I did this, those behind me did it, but in slow motion the house of cards caught up with me as I too fell to the ground, those behind me falling under me, those in front of me crushing me from above.

Like all near-death situations, this all proceeded in slow motion so I felt nothing like real panic. There was no point in freaking out since I was well and truly trapped. I thought that this was it. The real thing. For a while I couldn't breathe in a total darkness but then a little light appeared and my lungs filled up. I could make out the limbs and body parts of those on top of me. Then they seemed to float up off me and I saw that I was going to live. What seemed like the friendliest arms in the world reached out to save me. All strength was gone from my legs and arms, I couldn't get myself up, and my rescuers had to lift me back into the vertical.

Twenty people were allegedly taken to hospital after the Brixton gig with what were called general "pit" injuries. One girl set fire to her hair outside the venue. *The Times* said it was like a cross between *Starlight Express* and a full-scale riot. Which is exactly what it was like.

We Can Be Heroes – Berlin 2000

"I read somewhere that the personality of Berlin was pounded into the ashes of WWII and that Berliners so lack identity that they grasp at all your strong symbols and icons," says DJ More to me as he points out the apartment where Bowie and Iggy lived during their Berlin period. DJ More is a leftfield experimentalist and strong icons are something he knows quite a bit about. He DJed the aftershow parties on Michael Jackson's last tour. He is in his mid-twenties, old enough to give me a graphic account of the night the Wall came down.

"They could obviously see right into the East from their apartment," he says as we both stare up at the tall building where great songs were once written. We're standing on what would have been the other side of the Wall, not far from Prenzlauberg where the squatting, punk, and anarchist scenes are at their strongest. Recently militant anarchist vegans – the Molotov Moshers – attacked chi chi restaurants trying to open up in the district. They invaded the dining areas and proceeded to drench the patrons in animal blood which they carried around with them in large plastic buckets.

We head for the Sniper Bar where Alex Empire from Atari Teenage Riot hangs out when in town. Tonight the DJ is playing Digital Hardcore-style techno. In a cabinet containing a large number of punk and anarchist curiosities I note a photograph of Adolf Hitler, Eva Braun, and other worthies sitting in comfortable looking armchairs in a big sitting room.

"This looks like a real photograph," I say to More.

"It was grabbed from Hitler's apartment by the grandfather of somebody involved with the Sniper Bar," he says, though he doesn't have too much to say about it.

Atari Teenage Riot and their incendiary leader Alec Empire are both reflective of the noisy clamour of humanity that is Berlin, and one of the influences on that noise amongst young intellectually (and physically) energetic Berliners. When he formed the band in '92, rising out of the ashes of punk and techno, Empire said that they got together because they could no longer identify with techno, once a potent catalyst for musical and social change. They wanted to make music that was not subordinate to the dogmatic rules of the dancefloor. Disillusioned with the instrumental nature of techno, they were determined to install the specified nature of punk lyrics at the core of their work. Their tune 'Cyberpunks Are Dead' features the grinding sound of a backwards guitar borrowed from The Stooges.

> *"Digital Hardcore – that is to say guitar samples, distorted breakbeats, magna samples and shouting, very noisy. Riot sounds produce riots! We are left-radical. Anarchists perhaps, we do not want to change the system, we want to destroy it."*

Empire's fans all over the world seem to have taken into themselves the very essence of cranky German individualism. When I saw him DJ at a Digital Hardcore multiband bill he was subjected to a barrage of insults from his most rabid fans, a mixture of sexy girls, very young lonely planet boys, and older grizzled druggies. The accusations concerned the fact that Digital Hardcore was shifting a fair few units and that, in recent times, Atari Teenage Riot had signed to The Beastie Boys' Grand Royal label for America. This in turn lead to them appearing on a number of dubious mainstream American festival bills, sharing stages with acts as mellow as The Cardigans. To top off this controversial embracing of the American way, in '01 the band issued *Rage*, an EP featuring Tom Morello from Rage Against The Machine. While I watched Empire dropping his tunes the fans screamed "Capitalist pig!" and "Fucking exploiter!" at him. It was just like being in Berlin.

Empire defended his certain shift away from the grungy fringe empire where he ruled alone. His self-defense, that he was spreading the good word amongst the bad people, is the standard one given by radicals when they sell out.

> *"We are doing shows to incite people for action against the government, not to preach to the converted. We want to get this message of social equality out everywhere we can. Our shows are about confronting the audience with this . . . we don't have anything in common with the other bands; they suck . . . I don't want to judge them but we play everywhere – for example, big rock shows, underground shows, demonstrations, whatever."*

The owners of the Sniper Bar don't like people taking photographs of the Bar's interior, don't allow camcorders in there, and they don't want people giving media publicity to their place. Over hash cakes and mint tea we watch a screening of *Deathrace 2000*. We are joined by about ten others by the time we're thinking of heading for Syrie.

Getting to Syrie involves walking along the side of the Berlin Wall for about four kilometres. It's a pretty run-down part of town so endless amounts of the Wall still stand intact, covered with everything from Keith Haring-like tourist friendly paintings to political manifestos and photocopied posters for gigs and parties. There are loads of deserted office blocks, warehouses, and cheap hotels like the one which uses a photograph of Gorbachev kissing Hoenecker, the last Communist ruler of East Germany, on its headed notepaper.

The people walking with me are much the same age as

More. They're all ex-citizens of the East, and they all deeply resent the manner in which their society has been colonised by people with whom they feel no affinity. The alienation of East Berliners from the new order is profound. In the years immediately after reunification the title deeds to most city centre buildings were in flux. There was no paperwork available, and most of the properties had belonged to the GDR, the old Communist state which had gone up in a puff of smoke.

As a result of this confusion Prenzlauberg descended into becoming a virtually autonomous militant anarchist community right in the middle of Berlin. Bands and art galleries and experimental spaces shot up all over the place. Syrie, the club we're heading for, is one of the many places around that part of Berlin which still works to the extreme agenda of those days.

Its 3.30 a.m. by the time we reach Syrie, a large space reclaimed out of the ground floor of a huge Soviet-era office building which is about ten storeys high and runs for several blocks. On the walls outside posters for various Syrie gigs have been pasted up. It seems that, in addition to underground gigs like the one we're going to, a lot of acts who have good booking agencies and record deals of some sort play there.

Inside the foyer about five guys in their early twenties are standing around a counter and administration area. They're obviously staff, though they don't look any older or more prosperous than Syrie's patrons. About forty punks, many in couples, are strewn around on various reclaimed couches and armchairs. The girls are generally of the shocking pink mohawk and dodgy sunglasses variety. The guys come in several different sizes; S, M, L, and XL. They're from several different tribes including the mohawks, the thin rockist longhairs, and the just plain weird. Mainly teenagers, divided equally between the sexes, most of them drugged up on various trips. There had obviously been a big crowd there earlier in the night because the floor was covered in beer cans and flyers for music, politics, readings. I notice several flyers making mention of events organised by the Molotov Moshers.

Beyond the foyer large doors lead into the main hall, a spacious room with a big stage where about 200 people are moshing in the darkness to a fierce electronic thump very much in the Digital Hardcore style of howled lyrics over a vile, degenerate, series of electronic loops. There is a lot of dry ice around the stage area so I can't see the musicians. I walk through the crowd to get closer to the stage. I notice that the moshing is very intense and drug-fuelled. The vast majority of the moshers are spaced out a good distance from one another. They're sweating, caught up in worlds of their own, and have the appearance of having moshed for hours.

There is something approaching a crowd up near the stage. Here there is a tendency for nine or ten individuals to tornado in on top of each other with real nerve and verve. Like people doing the Hokey Cokey on acid. The age groups here are 15–20 and passing through them is like going through electricity. The music they're reacting against is being played by three long haired guys in all kinds of clothes standing in front of three laptops which are spread out on a long old-fashioned deal table. They're very much caught up in their computers, oblivious to the mayhem their music is creating out there in the ice and smoke.

There is a fair amount of aggression near the stage, but it's entirely physical. The music pulsates with so much muscle that the connection between rhythm and body is total. A blond kid, about eighteen, taps me on the shoulder and gives me the cupped hands sign. He wants me to lift him up so that he can surf in the pit. This strikes me as being a daft idea but I always take the "Let them off!" approach to everything that happens in the pit. So I cup my hands, he put his Vans trainer into the cup, and I heave him heftily up onto the pit where the moshers get a kick out of catching him and holding him aloft for five minutes before he reaches the stage and dances around the preoccupied band.

About an hour later I'm having a coffee in the foyer of Syrie when the blond kid comes out of the hall, on his way home with his girlfriend. His name is Kuhl, his girlfriend Ilko. I note that she is wearing one of several Molotov Mosher T-shirts I've seen at Syrie. Kuhl says he likes terrorism in his music. "I came to anarchism through techno. Then I came to moshing through anarchism." He says that all the scenes are very connected in on one another, that the people you'd meet in a mosh pit would be the same people active in feminist groups or strange art projects or the Molotov Moshers. "I think the Molotov thing may be more of a concept than a reality," he laughs, looking over at Ilko. I ask him does he mean the moshing scene in general, or the one connected in on sort of squat scenes like the one in Syrie.

"Here in the East, there is mainly this kind of moshing which is anti-sexist and anti-racist and part of a whole range of social and so on activities. If the term Molotov Moshers means anything real, that is what it means, a collective sense. The other scene, the nu-metal commercial scene, that exists everywhere now but not on this side of town so much. Alec Empire had a great influence here where he came from, and also he was a very typical Berlin artist. The punks are in the front line of opposition so there is such a scene of very real punk bands. That band you saw tonight is one type, that I really like. But there are hundreds of small drums, bass guitar punk bands playing in cellars or the courtyards of big squats or even sometimes in places like this. Russian punk bands. I like all that stuff. This show tonight would have been in listings and have posters up around Prenzlauberg but a lot of the best gigs you just get the flyers in

certain cafes and clubs or even people will come on word of mouth because most things are free or just a donation. The punk scene here is physically real tough and hardcore. They're kind of in the front line in the war against the Nazis who, of course, have also gathered around a kind of hardcore. And ska and other things."

Kuhl, befuddled by the illogic of racists listening to black music, laughs and turns to his girlfriend to whom he says, "Oh, fuck, it is crazy! Those Nazis are fucking crazy!"

He makes his farewells, and I head back into the hall where DJ More and pals are the only people on the floor dancing happily. The same band seemed, so far as I could tell, to be playing the exact same tune. When we departed around 6 a.m. the room was still vibrating with their raw irregular beat. There were loads of new people arriving as we left.

A Hole In The Crowd – Roskilde '99

Roskilde Festival was founded in '71 as a kind of Danish Woodstock. In the early days bands playing over two days would draw about 20,000 people. Most of those bands being best forgotten Scandinavian "progressive" outfits with the occasional UK superstar act like The Kinks thrown in for glamour. As the years went by Roskilde grew and grew. Never a hardcore or even particularly contemporary festival, headliners in the years leading up to the Pearl Jam disaster included R.E.M. and Neil Young. Quality high ticket acts, but not exactly cutting edge or walking on the wild side. All profits from the festival went to a variety of good causes like Amnesty and Human Rights Watch.

By 2000 there were 70,000 people buying weekend tickets for the bash. About 50,000 of these gathered in front of the Orange Stage around 10.30 p.m. on June 30 to catch Pearl Jam, old school rock'n'roll crowd pleasers. They'd emerged out of the innovative early Nineties Seattle scene. In recent years they've worked with Old Guy superstars like The Who, Bob Dylan, and Neil Young.

In keeping with the good vibes and hippy spirit which gave birth to the festival, Roskilde's perimeter fence was not the usual concentration-camp style barbed wire and metal sheeting we associate with festivals in fields, but a string of trees. Leif Skov, one of the partners running the festival for decades,

147

defended the trees: "That's part of our security. It keeps people positive and controlled. We don't carry weapons. We carry a smile."

The festival had twelve full-time staff and, in 2000, there were an amazing 17,000 volunteers working on the event. When asked if these people were ill-equipped to deal with the tragedy, Skov said philosophically (perhaps too philosophically): "What proper education is there for security? In Denmark there isn't any. Their 'education' is experience. And preparation."

Professionals present on the site that day – travelling with international acts on the summer festival circuit – agree that things were organised with traditional Scandinavian efficiency and common sense. Roskilde was justifiably proud of its track record. It had no great reputation for trouble or violence. They were presenting a mixed bill, not something centred around the now ubiquitous summer festival agenda of hardcore, skacore and nu-metal. Ironically enough, one of the very few moments of publicised violence associated with Roskilde before the '99 disaster also involved Pearl Jam.

During a '92 set by the group, vocalist Eddie Vedder was at the centre of a substantial confrontation when he saw a stage-diver getting rough treatment from bouncers in the pit. Vedder jumped off the stage and got into a violent scuffle with security who claimed not to know who he was and punched him. According to some accounts Vedder was hit hard.

Pearl Jam enjoyed a strong reputation as a band who took care of their fans out in the pit. They'd always insisted that the kids could both mosh and live to tell the tale. They'd initiated an informed policy of employing their own pit crew, street smart music fans who kept an eye on what was happening. They were an integral part of the Nirvana/Sub Pop/Dinosaur Jr. scene which helped kickstart moshing in the first place.

In '93 Pearl Jam cancelled a performance at the University of Colorado because the authorities barred moshing. In '95, when the whole moshing thing was exploding all over America, the band's tour security director advised concert industry professionals that at "The shows we do today you'll see security headbanging, you'll see them actually volunteering to get up and body surf with the audience – I'll ask them to do it. You'll also see us in the mosh pit, moshing with the kids."

On the subject of hiring locals to do security at concerts and festivals, Pearl Jam's security director told the gathered professionals a lot about the band's general attitude: "How many people here use drug rehab kids for their security in-house? Not too many, huh? I didn't think so. One of the things I've asked is: go down to these drug rehabs, show some of these kids that we're not forgetting about them. Let them turn their lives around . . . To say they were involved in a concert that night, or a basketball game, or a hockey game means a lot to them."

When they played their home town, Seattle, their manager and some band members went to security meetings at the Seattle Center before the show and participated in discussions about what the systems were. According to the *Seattle Post-Intelligencer*, a former deputy director of the Center said that Pearl Jam wanted to know about "how we were going to handle people coming over the barricades and how we were going to talk to people. It's pretty rare that specific band members get involved in that much detail."

Pearl Jam's debut album, *Ten*, sold more than 2,000,000 copies. In the eight years between Vedder's '92 Roskilde intervention and 2000 Pearl Jam ceased to be post-Seattle freaks with firm roots in new music and aesthetics. They were in danger of turning into one more stadium rock beast out there on the circuit perpetuating their own mythology. They were no longer popular with hip and grungy kids who can survive in any pit. They *did* remain political. In the lead up to the 2000 election Vedder called George W. Bush "Damien II".

A volunteer security officer on duty for the Pearl Jam show, Per Johansen, was the first to report the catastrophe about to unravel. Stationed some ten feet to the left of stage centre, he noticed that the crowd was very big and strangely tense. The tension he sensed upfront was no doubt caused by people's realisation that the crowd was way too big and that they were all moving imperceptibly but remorselessly forward. "It was really crowded but not dangerous," Johansen told the media. "We'd had that size of a crowd before and there was no problem."

Jo Markham, a Lollapalooza veteran, in love with the pungent odour of travelling/hardcore festivals in America, ended up at Roskilde by accident. It was not her normal type of show. She was not as complacent as Per Johansen when Pearl Jam came on.

"I guess I was less worked up then than some of the people around me. Maybe because that was the case I saw more of the bad stuff that was happening. Normally European festivals are way more chill than their US counterparts and the culture of going to festivals every summer is a much more social thing. In America you go to a festival to get pissed or stoned . . . to grab some ass. I think people go to European shows to actually hear the music. But it was real cold, cold damp, and Scandinavian that day at Roskilde. The atmosphere was dreadful. You had a lot of these really burly and aggressive German guys, sinister macho types, remorselessly infiltrating the mosh pit area. There was never going to be any moshing anyway. It was way too tight packed in the first place. Secondly, and this is important, the only people who were going to want to mosh at Pearl Jam were going to be bozos who had no experience of the pit, who'd seen it on MTV pop promos or read all about it in the papers."

As Pearl Jam, a mighty live band, worked their way into their set Per Johansen noticed that something was wrong. "There were some girls who were extremely difficult to pull up out of the mosh pit. Usually, it takes one guy to pull one up. But we needed two."

It seems that it was difficult for anybody, including Pearl Jam, to see what was happening in the pit. They subsequently complained about poor visibility of the audience from the stage. The centrifugal sway of the tight-packed fans was knocking people off balance and down onto the ground where arms and legs were getting tangled in on one another to create a human spaghetti junction where it was impossible for people to maintain their physical autonomy. One guy, about 15 feet back from the stage, reported to the media: "I saw people start to fall. I could still see their heads but they were much lower than the rest of us. A guy in front of me saw the problems they were having and said, 'Push the other way.' We did this three times but it didn't help."

Nineteen-year-old Thomas Miller confirmed that it was tight in the pit long before Pearl Jam went on: "People were stumbling left and right. Half an hour in I knew it was life or death. I couldn't lift up my arms. It was difficult to breathe. I lifted my head to feel clean air. I was scared for my life." A 22-year-old familiar with Roskilde – he'd been there seven times previously – said: "There was too much pressure in there. It was like I was standing at a crossroads. People wanting to get to the front were putting their hands on each other's shoulders and squeezing through. It felt aggressive. I stayed five songs and then pushed my way out."

Jo Markham spent the first twenty minutes of Pearl Jam talking to people all around her, trying to calm them down and telling them to organise themselves.

"There were a lot of really uncool people in there. I got groped a few times but I've been groped before and like a lot of people who are into moshing, I have kind of mutated notions about my own

physical space so I'm not too put out by a little casual nonsense. There were also some very strait-laced people in there who should have been way back from the stage area, and then there were these out of control bozos. I felt that their intentions were gross. An ex-boyfriend of mine got a broken arm and crushed ribs at a Slipknot gig in LA so I know all about this kind of shit . . . I was trying to calm people down but it was totally out of control. I would say that what happened was not because of any one factor. Shit happens. Especially within the context of rock'n'roll. I guess that shit is part of the edge that keeps it interesting. The edge was sex way back in my mom's time. Then it was sex and drugs. Now its all that and we need something else in the mix too to give us a little edge. After what I saw at Roskilde I had plenty of reasons to reflect on things."

An 18-year-old girl told the Danish paper *Politiken* that she had pals near the stage who were "standing on one of the poor people. They thought it was bags. When they saw that it was a person lying on the ground they couldn't get off." Another woman told the same paper that she saw five people standing on a man and that she tried to pull him up: "I went crazy and yelled, 'Move, move, he's got to get up.' But they didn't move even though they must have sensed they were standing on him. I can't remember his face or anything but I can remember that he was looking at me. Then it was over. I think he died."

Around 11.15 p.m. Per Johansen says he turned to his security chief and asked her to stop the music, telling her: "I think people are dead." He claims that he repeated this request twice and then another member of the pit crew made the same request. The message went up the chain of command, eventually reaching Pearl Jam's tour manager standing on the side of the stage. He made his way onto the stage to tell Eddie Vedder what was going on.

Vedder got the band to stop playing and spoke to the crowd. The advice he gave that crowd was advice that responsible bands give crowds all over the world when things start getting a bit dodgy: "What will happen in the next five minutes has nothing to do with music. But it is important. Imagine that I am your friend and that you must step back so as not to hurt me. You all have friends up front. I will now count to three, and you will all take three steps back. All who agrees say 'Yes' now." This brought a big cheer from the crowd and a minor backwards movement. Vedder made his request one more time. A journalist for *Pollstar*, the US concert industry magazine, who was in the audience said: "You could really see when the crowd moved back. It looked like they really moved a couple of feet back."

Jo Markham wasn't quite so sure. "Yeah they did move back a bit," she murmurs, "but then like lemmings they moved forward again. It was more like one step backwards, then two steps forward. This was not deliberate asshole behaviour. Just that with so many people, the sheer bulk of the crowd was in control. Not Eddie Vedder or the bouncers."

Promoter Leif Skov ran to the security area, and saw what was going on about seven feet from the front fence: "I saw there was a hole in the crowd – where there were no heads."

At the bottom of this hole, about seven feet in diameter, there was a pile of young bodies. Security leaped into the crowd and passed victims over the barrier where they were carried backstage for medical treatment. The backstage medical team was overwhelmed by the numbers they had to deal with and by the severity of the injuries. An English tour manager took it upon himself to clear an area full of trucks so that accident victims could be swiftly moved. Some say that 15 minutes elapsed between the time when Per Johansen sent his warning to his superior and when the music stopped but organiser Skov says: "He's right that his message had to travel to various people. But he's not right about the time it takes. We are not using telephones. We're not running around with messages. We are using walkie-talkies."

Some people say that the cause of the intense surges and crushes was the bad quality of the sound coming from the delay towers designed to give a decent sound to those at the back of the crowd. According to this theory people moved forward to hear better. Another witness says that even up front the sound was "all treble and too quiet. It sounded so wrong." But complaints about poor sound quality are part and parcel of middle-of-the-road rock gigs. You don't hear punk rockers complaining about the quality of the sound too often. Folk who attend gigs like Roskilde tend to be very occasional concert goers, content with the sound of their CDs on domestic rack systems in their suburban homes but unfamiliar with the rough and ready raw sound of live music blasting out at you in a field in the middle of nowhere.

Others put it all down to the rain, this theory being that the ground was turned to mush so that people were slipping and sliding all over the place. This *does* happen a lot when it rains on festivals, and mucky mosh pits are a frightening, risky business. The Roskilde site, sometimes used for agricultural shows, is on farmland, its perimeters dotted with cattle sheds. On the day, the cold miserable drizzle turned some parts of the site into mud but there was not a lot of mud around the Orange Stage where the carnage took place. The ground immediately in front of the stage had been paved with "stone flour", a mixture of clay and sand that drains water away quickly. Stone flour is impressively effective in all but the most extreme situations.

The site was peppered with overturned u-shaped metal barriers sunk deep into the ground. These impediments were the norm in English soccer stadiums until it was decided in the Eighties that they were responsible for rib and other injuries.

Paul Wertheimer, head of the Chicago company Crowd Management Strategies, a vocal no-nonsense campaigner against poor crowd control and mosh pit culture, says that these barriers might have worked OK with a smaller crowd but at Roskilde "they certainly weren't helpful. They probably complicated matters when the chain reaction went into play."

A press photographer who didn't particularly like Pearl Jam recalled that he "saw no laughing in that crowd. There was no joy on their faces. You could see people were not happy." He left the performance before things turned sour but returned when he heard what was going on. "I saw a police officer shouting to people – so small and so alone. He was trying to get people to move back. Shouting at a huge crowd. It illustrates how hopeless it all was."

A 26-year-old police cadet from Germany, a 23-year-old man from Holland, three Swedes and three Danes all died of asphyxiation at the scene. A ninth man, an Australian, was hospitalised with chest injuries and attached to an artificial respirator. He died a few days later.

Eddie Vedder sat on the stage, gazing into the black hole where the dead people lay, his face appearing on a vast video screen erected right behind the mixing desk tower. He was visibly crying.

By 1.05 a.m. the Roskilde organisers were telling the crowd that the next band due on – The Cure – was cancelled. Music on all the other stages went ahead, with some bands starting as late as 3 a.m. At the time of the tragedy Underworld were on the techno stage while Brit indie band Travis were elsewhere in the same field. Given the scale of the carnage, this business-as-usual approach was the first manifestation of the organiser's notion that, in traditional showbiz style, the show must go on.

That night in his hotel room Vedder wrote a statement which was issued to the media in the middle of the night: "We have not yet been told what actually occurred, but it seemed random and sickeningly quick ... it doesn't make sense. When you agree to play a festival of this size and reputation, it is impossible to imagine such a heart-wrenching scenario."

A month after the deaths Pearl Jam issued a more thoughtful and defensive statement indicating that they'd thought a lot about the awful things they saw in Denmark. In the weeks since the festival there'd been efforts on the part of local police to lay the blame for what went wrong at their door. There were murmurings about the band being "morally responsible" for it all. Pearl Jam have always been ballsy political players, once attempting to challenge Ticketmaster's stranglehold on US ticket sales. Now, their backs to the wall, they said that they were determined to get to the bottom of the Roskilde conundrum.

They wanted to see a thorough investigation of "chain-of-command for Festival security ... We stopped the show immediately upon being informed that there might be a problem, even though we were asked to wait until the nature of the problem could be determined. It is our belief that if we'd been informed of a potential problem at the moment that it was first identified by the Festival security, we could have stopped the show earlier and lives could have been saved." They were also critical of the medical facilities backstage, saying there was "a lack of adequate and/or necessary qualified technicians, emergency medical equipment, and ambulances to quickly and adequately address medical emergencies."

The band cancelled the last few gigs of their six week European trek, went into seclusion when they returned to the US, but proceeded with plans to tour American arenas and amphitheatres a month later. By November, when they played the Seattle Key Arena, they were complaining to the audience about the gig having too much safety and security. At the same time their marketing minders set about presenting an image of them as a band permanently concerned about mosh pit safety.

"During the performance, participants moved around the undefined centre of the 'pit' like some great hurricane of youthful exuberance and anger. As members danced they competed with one another, but also with the larger community who defined the boundaries of the dance area." Riot sounds produce riots. Evil Fest 2000 at Underworld, Camden, London. (*Neil Massey/PYMCA*)

Iggy takes the plunge to the delight of the ladies. (*Michael Ochs Archives/Redferns*)

The Ramones, kings of punk, inventing the moshpit. (*LFI*)

ourtney Love, low slung guitar heroine, prepares to dip into the population at Glastonbury '99. (*LFI*)

Stage diver wearing appropriate pants and shoes. (*Martyn Goodacre*/SIN)

Young New York hardcore slamdancers, '92. (*David Corio*/SIN)

Back in the vintage days, Albuquerque '90. (*Derek Ridgers/PYMCA*)

Red Hot Chilli Peppers at the ongoing peak of their powers, Seattle 2000. (*LFI*)

Bad Brains worshipping the Almighty. It was Bad Brains, mashing down Babylon, who started the talk about moshing. (*Peter Anderson/SIN*)

America's finest youth at Woodstock '99 (*Richard Beland/SIN*)

A lean and mean '92 Eddie Vedder (*Anita Bugge*/*SIN*)

Mate Feed Kill Repeat. Slipknot prepares to release their virus. Joey Jordison is on the far right.
(*Grant Davis/Redferns*)

Good guys? One Minute Silence tattoo you, 2000.
(*Tony Wooliscroft/Idols*)

Dread metal goes back to the primitive. Max Cavalera,
ex-Sepultura and now Soulfly, London Astoria '98. (*LFI*)

"The best pits were the ones where people were about your own age and build. You got pushed around but it wasn't a hard push. You have to go into the pit with a certain attitude to moshing. When you're psyched up about a band anyway, and you get the chance to see them live, you get *really* psyched up beforehand about going into the pit." Evil Fest, 2000 (*Neil Massey/PYMCA*)

A sympathetic interview with guitarist Mike McCready in their local rag, the *Seattle Post-Intelligencer*, reported that: "The group has used a customised barrier with padded railings to provide a buffer between the stage and the mosh pit." McCready said that they'd considered breaking up after Roskilde but "It wouldn't have been a good way to end it all . . . We realised we're making viable music. We can't stop. We can't end on a down note."

"It's about the worst thing that can happen to a rock band," McCready told the *Intelligencer*. "People shouldn't have to die at rock concerts."

In a posting to his website Who leader Pete Townshend, who'd seen eleven people die in a stampede before his band's '79 Cincinnati show, wrote about a phone conversation he had with Vedder not long after Roskilde: "I passed on what I knew The Who had done wrong after the Cincinnati disaster – in a nutshell I think we left too soon and I spoke too angrily to the press and without proper consideration for the fact that the people who deserved respect were the dead and their families."

Townshend was referring to an interview he gave to *Rolling Stone* in '80, the year after the deaths at Cincinnati. In that interview he gave voice to what must often be the attitude of bands on the road.

> *"It was, 'Fuck it!' We're not going to let a little thing like this stop us. That was the way we had to think. We had to reduce it . . . We had a tour to do. We're a rock'n'roll band. You know we don't fuck around, worrying about twelve people dying. We care about it, but there is a particular attitude I call 'tour armour'. When you go on the road you throw up an armour around your- self, you almost go into a trance."*

The morning after the Roskilde tragedy concert promoter Skov called a press conference at which he announced that the festival would go ahead as planned. "Life," he declared, "is stronger than death." Two English pop bands – Pet Shop Boys and Oasis – refused to go along with this. Management for both bands issued a statement calling on the Roskilde organisers to cancel performances on the Orange Stage to facilitate the investigation and out of respect for the dead. They also cited fear about safety at the gig. The local police had completed their on-site investigations and declared themselves happy that the show should go on. Oasis said they didn't particularly feel like singing 'Live Forever' in the context and Pet Shop Boys said they were doing a greatest hits party set. Leader Neil Tennant commented: "To do that on a site where eight people had just died seemed inconceivable."

Roskilde were none too happy about acts pulling out and announced that, in their opinion, "the bands that decided to follow through with their concerts on the existing and approved conditions show both respect and consideration to the dead." They subsequently admitted that "some words were said that should not have been said", wrote to the bands in question to apologise, and told *Rolling Stone* that they wanted to put both band's fees into a Roskilde 2000 Tragedy Fund for the study of safety and security. Having cited the anguish of the bereaved as one of their reasons for withdrawing from the festival, Pet Shot Boys were snappy enough when told they were not going to get paid. "There was no communication between them and our agent on that," Neil Tennant told *Rolling Stone.*

Six months after the disaster Leif Skov announced the first of Roskilde's efforts to ensure that things would be better in future. He said that at one stage the organisers had considered abandoning the festival entirely. "All we ever seek to do is to make places where young people can go and hear music and have a good time. It would have been so easy to react too strongly, to put up severe militant fencing but that wouldn't necessarily have been safer."

"The problem has been that there is no one guilty party. There were no violent people to blame," he said. Announcing new strategies which would be in place for Roskilde 2001, when the bill featured safer Old Guy acts like Bob Dylan and Neil Young, Skov said: "We'll have stewards in the crowds, constantly walking round to assess when the maximum number of people who can stand safely has been reached. Then we can stop access to that area of the festival before anything bad happens."

Skov announced that they'd had many proposals for statues to be erected on the site bearing the names and birth-dates of the kids who'd died. They decided that this would be too much and, instead, planned to plant a circle of nine trees with stones between them, where people could sit and get away from the crowds. "There'll be a big stone in the centre of the circle with some appropriate wording on it," he said. "It will be established once the frost is off the ground in the early spring."

Mosh Pit Bandits – The Kids Are All White

Alex went to hundreds of gigs. He usually had a bite mark on his shoulder, a bloody gash in one of his ears, or a love bite on his neck. He was always sardonic and sceptical about the bands he was looking at. He didn't buy their merchandise-flogging rhetoric or their insistence that "you guys are the best crowd we've played to" but he loved moshing more than most. He kept a log of the small shows and out of town shows he'd attended. He would travel long distances to see some small American skapunk collective doing a show in a Brighton squat. About five foot ten and lightly built, he had a big wardrobe of cool clothes.

He removed everything but his jeans and sneakers before going into the pit. All his other clothes would be neatly packed up in his shoulder bag and deposited in the cloakroom. He moved energetically in the pit where he had great staying power, being full of skill and sublimated anger.

> *"I have a passion for keeping a little violence in my life. I always have had since puberty. I'm 19 now, I work for an advertising agency, a kind of shitty job as their in-house courier. The first pit I ever went into was for The Rollins Band. I laugh when I look back on it now because I've gone totally off that kind of stuff. I think a lot of people come to moshing by unexpected paths, listening to music that later embarrasses them. You go to some act in the area of music you think you like – in my case it was all those*

160

smart American post punk and hardcore guys . . . Rollins, Sonic Youth, Fugazi, Beasties. I was way into that level of music. I think you come into moshing via any kind of generic heavy energetic music. Most come from metal and hardcore but loads come in and join us from indie and hip-hop scenes too.

"If moshing catches you by the balls and you get hooked on it, you begin to drift away from whatever music brought you to that place in your life, and you end up liking bands you can mosh to. I don't mean that you end up liking just any band you can use for moshing though that shit happens too. You meet new people with whom you seem to share so much in common and they tell you about CDs or they arrange to meet you for a drink before some forthcoming gig. The next thing you know you're on the fringes of a scene, which is somewhere I never imagined being because I'm a serious loner and I despise movements like punk or skinhead. I like being alone and I'm not too sure of myself in the company of others, particularly women.

"The pit made me a lot less formal and self-important, more flexible about the needs of others. Around '99 there were maybe 300 of us who'd meet up in groups of eight or nine at the Virgin Megastore before gigs in The Astoria or in Camden on Saturday afternoons to talk bullshit. Then we might go to the Electric Ballroom for the Full Tilt club which was dire but there was nowhere else to go. A lot of the others were still at school although I'd already quit. I was out there in the big bad world so I didn't necessarily have too much in common with their values. By which, I guess, I mean that I wanted to be a loner again.

"But through all that socialising and meeting up with new people in the pit every time I went, I did meet some nice girls who liked the bands I was getting into then such as NOFX or Rancid. It was around that time that I started sussing out the underground, which involved me getting on loads of mailing lists, and getting to see a lot of gigs you never hear about in London. I started travelling to festivals in Germany. Always there was an *adventure involved with that kind of thing, and I found that I was getting to see much more interesting bands. When you're at the mercy of commercial promoters who have to pay insurance, hire bouncers, come on with all that professional shit, you're missing the real deal. I always liked the pit for the music, the sense you get in the pit that music couldn't get any better. I know this is an experience moshers share with ravers, though most moshers I know are not full-time druggies.*

"People go on about moshing being a male thing. There is a lot of talk about all that sweating male flesh being a kind of queer vibe. I've never noticed anything like that but then I wouldn't. You also hear about queer sex in the pit but I've never noticed that either and I think I would. You do see cute little moments going on between boys and girls and you do see girls getting their tits squeezed without their permission. Nobody likes that. To some extent I know what they mean when they say moshing is a male thing but I don't think its fair to suggest that women are not welcome – or are made unwelcome – in the pit. A lot of the bands I go to, I never noticed problems of that sort. It was always cool to help girls up to surf. Especially cute girls. Moshing could some-times be a good way of meeting girls for sure.

"On the other hand, it is a fact of life that the pit is rough and some women can't handle that or disapprove of it. They must make up their own minds. A lot of women obviously think they're missing out on the fun, so they leap into the middle of the pit and find themselves in deep, deep trouble. So its 'Let me in, let me in.' And then the minute they're in its 'Let me out, let me out.' I know that on paper it seems outrageous that the pit can be such an all-male thing but there are loads of other activities in life where women don't get too involved. I know there are some women boxers but boxing is mainly a guy's thing. The same applies to football, loads of other recreations. I love having women in the pit but they need to be able to look after themselves. Nobody else is going to give a fuck what happens to them."

The sports analogy is pertinent. A lot of the guys you meet in the pit in America are in peak physical condition and have put as many hours into polishing their tricks and techniques as athletes or dancers. In circles where people mosh in clubs to rock or industrial DJs there has been a noticeable drift away from moshing as we know it. From the late Eighties on dancers were checking out moshing and its movements. There were people in there taking mental notes on the chaos, assessing the self-sustaining community at its core.

There is now a small elite of moshers who go around the world behaving like snow boarders, self-appointed ego-driven jocks who think they've invented a lifestyle for themselves. They've added contours to the crude moves and shapes they first saw in the pit. Now they call their unique read on moshing "technique-based moshing". It is sometimes hard to understand what these guys are going on about for they speak an exclusivist jargon. It is arguable that they stand opposed to everything that is good about moshing.

Dylan Hales is a leading technique-based mosher:

"It was first introduced to me in around '92 when I first saw some videos of hardcore shows in the Northeastern part of the US. At that time I thought it just looked like a bunch of guys trying to kill each other. But I've always been a big advocate of unnecessary violence, so I decided I might have a future in this art form. I can't say I can honestly recall the first time I was in a highly organised pit but I do recall several times in the seventh and eighth grade that myself and some other punkers did the mosh at recess. I also attempted to circle pit around a table once in science class that year, which resulted in a firm scolding from Mrs Spainhour. It is a definite toss-up whether my best move is the running handspring flip into an 'accidental' kick, or the full rotation windmill into a spin kick. I believe myself to be the originator of this move as myself and the Orator of Mosh Bubba have

examined tapes and have yet to find anyone who can claim this move as part of his or her repertoire.

"The mosh has caused many a busted sore knuckle and broken toe amongst other atrocities but I'm sure that as the technological age advances onward these injuries will be replaced with positive attitudes and post-show hugs. I think that moshing should be an Olympic sport. I mean gymnastics has a floor exercise that with some slight alterations could easily be converted into a mosh exercise. Moshers train just as hard as other athletes, and they deserve to be recognised as more than just your run-of-the-mill thugs. I can only hope that there is a future in the Olympics but I'm afraid many moshers would decline invitations if professional moshers were allowed in on the proceedings. I guess the best way to explain why I mosh would be to quote professional wrestling legend Terry Funk (my personal hero): 'In the beginning of time there were three original sports. You either ran for survival, swam for survival, or fought for survival.' Moshing is a form of fighting that takes out the middle man, i.e. the guy who is getting hurt. Sure its showing off but who cares. Baseball players show off and so do basketball players. Do their respective communities admonish them? Of course not. So don't admonish the mosh, respect and treat it well, for it will do the same to you in the long run."

Matt, a dapper little guy with a chirpy sense of humour, comes from New England. He grew up in the late Eighties, oppressed by heavy metal and by the culture of sports:

"I come from a small town of about 10,000 people. All these rednecks used to come into town in their trucks and vans in the evenings and on Saturdays. They'd have a rifle over the dashboard, car stereo going full blast, they were real assholes. For me, because this is what I was seeing, rock music was something you just wanted nothing whatsoever to do with. These guys were listening to Guns'n'Roses, Iron Maiden, Metallica so if it was

good enough for them then it was something I wanted nothing to do with. My mother whom I lived with along with my two brothers was a Christian so, until I broke loose, I was raised as a shy and reserved boy.

"The very sight of the rednecks driving by with Axl Rose screaming 'Live And Let Die' used to drive me into a frustrated rage. I felt so impotent, like there was something wrong with me as a man. As a reaction against that culture I was totally into techno. I loved techno and the drugs going with it. I still do. Used to pick up all my girlfriends at techno. I have these fond memories of techno because it was my first escape route out of the world I was living in. I quit college about two months into my first year and eventually – four months later – moved into a house in San Francisco. I had this girlfriend Judy who was two years older than me, I was about sixteen at the time, this was around '96 or '97. Judy was into the punk scene which I could see straight away was going somewhere other than that whole jock dude shit. We used to listen to X and Fugazi a lot so I ended up going to lots of hardcore gigs. Not all the bands I saw were good and my distaste for certain rockist attitudes was confirmed by things I saw.

"I guess my first experiences of going into a mosh pit are similar to most other guys. I sniffed around the edges for a long time, I was really terrified, which in a sense was the start of the addiction. Moshing can be the ultimate adolescent thrill, the fear of the slightly dangerous. This terror of the violence combines with a natural sense of intrigue. Any fool could see that those fucking people in the pit were obviously having fun. You want to be in there but you're afraid. That's the yin and yang of moshing. It has a good and a bad side so I guess it's a good training for life.

"Eventually I dipped my toe in the water. It was this big open-air festival where Red Hot Chili Peppers were playing. There sure were a lot of fucking awful jocks and sports guys at that gig but the Peppers are good people. The Peppers may be popular and *inconsistent but they've got good hearts, they're coming from a good place. I noticed that day that they didn't allow shit to go down in the crowd, they were taking care of business. I felt I trusted them so I plunged right in. It was like smoking for the first time or fucking for the first time. I didn't have all that great a time, I got hurt a bit, but I was in love with the whole fucking thing.*

"So I was back in the pit the next opportunity I got, about a week later, a show by Slayer. I remember every minute of that night. It was a real fucking howling at the moon night for me. I think the secret is to lose your fear of being injured, and the only way to do that is to endure a few scratches. I don't mean I'm positively into getting battered but as soon as you lose the fear of pain, you can move freely around the pit. You become a man on your own two feet. No boss, no girlfriend, no old pals, just you in the midst of impossible energy. I loosened up a great deal over the course of that hour and a half and when I went home that looseness stayed with me. At least some small part of it. So then I was off!

"For about the next year I was scanning all the listings looking for bands, and I had a whole new life. You get to have too much of a good thing so I pulled out and moved on. But I get back into the scene all the time. I think it gets more and more dangerous all the time. I say dangerous not violent – the point has always been that it should be violent. The danger is caused by forces beyond our control. The rise of certain crass bands like Limp Bizkit and Linkin Park and Papa Roach, the media obsession since people have died has brought every kind of fool and jerk known to man into the pit, the sheer popularity of punk and hardcore bands causing these huge crowds. Most festivals are going right over to punk/metal/hardcore. The Unplugged Era is well and truly over."

Mario works for a design studio in Soho while waiting for his painting career to take off. In his late twenties, he lives with five others in an Italian anarchist squat in Brixton. There are a few ragged punk bands on the fringes of his scene but the lethal combination of beer and heroin seems to keep them out of action most of the time. Mario himself is pretty distant from the others in his squat; their style is not necessarily his. He likes The Deftones, Slipknot, Atari Teenage Riot, and Revolting Cocks. He has enough money to go to a lot of gigs:

"My favourite venue in the whole world is the Brixton Academy. I liked it long before I moved to London. When I was fourteen I came with my big brother to see The Ramones at the Academy. So now I'm living around the corner from it and I go there every chance I can. I go to about two gigs a week, sometimes nothing when there's nothing on. Other times of the year, especially the autumn, it gets real busy. Sometimes I could be out six nights in a row, after which I'm totally fucked.

"I've been going out to gigs a long time now, five years, and I'm friendly with other people who do the same thing. I sometimes meet them on the streets and that can be strange. They can be really embarrassed to see you because people get up to all sorts of weird shit in the pit. It gets dark in there and people are really spinning into outer space. So you're seeing the people who are sharing the pit with you at their most extreme, when they're straining every muscle in their body to defend themselves. If you run into them on the street it can sometimes seem like you've done sex or drugs together. I have had sexual experiences in the pit with both men and women. Nothing worth worrying my girlfriend about!

"So you run into your mosh buddies in someplace civilised like a coffee shop or a bar in Brixton. They're there with their girlfriends, or other pals, and very often those people – their real everyday friends – have nothing to do with the music scene or that kind of extreme stuff. You share an intimate secret with the dude from the pit but, outside of that secret world, maybe you don't have a thing in common with him. That's strange.

"Since I've started spending all that time in the pit I've gotten fitter and stronger. In itself moshing is the very best kind of whole body exercise like swimming or cycling. Beyond that unintentional exercise that goes with the territory you have to take good care of yourself in your everyday life if you want to get the full value out of the pit. If you're going to suffer from the heat or the lack of oxygen when it gets real intense in the mosh, if you're going to be in physical trouble after 15 minutes, then you're never going to be a mosh pit bandit, someone who gets the maximum thrill from being there.

"If the gig is in Brixton this is my drill. I get home from work around 5.30. Uptown I wear a lot of sports gear which costs a bit but that gear I leave at home when I'm moshing. I've fucked up so many nice pieces of clothes in the pit that now I have a special selection of rags I keep separate from everything else. This stuff I wear moshing is not designed to make me look cool, it's just fucked up old stuff I keep for that purpose. It doesn't matter how torn or fucked up it gets. I like to wear combat trousers in the pit because they give you loads of pockets in which to safely stash away valuables like your watch and Travelcard and cash money. Also combat trousers are very durable and, you know, built for combat . . . which is what you're about to enter into. I would say that at certain bands, the mosh pit must be exactly what it was like in the trenches during W.W.I. Chaos everywhere, mud, blood, things coming at you from all angles. I also like to keep a fresh T-shirt in one of the pockets of the combats. I shower before I go, get dressed, drink some chilled fruit juice.

"You sweat so much that it's good to go wash your torso in the Academy toilets immediately after the band. I dry myself under the hand dryer. It's always like a cross between a dressing room and a stinky hairdressing salon in the toilets. Guys gasping for water, hand dryers going full blast, guys changing into fresh clothes. When I've got my nice, clean, fresh T-shirt put on I feel like a king. For shoes I keep two clapped-out old pairs of Nike Air

Walk trainers. They're good for giving you traction on the ground, they're comfortable, and they have loads of padding which protects your feet from all the stomping that goes on in the pit. The laces don't tend to come untied too much either. Losing shoes in the pit is common and fucks you up for the rest of the night. The Air Walks, principally, keep you both feet on the ground. Which if you ask me is the secret of successful moshing. If your feet give way, of course, you're fucked.

"When I get home afterwards every stitch on me right down to my boxer shorts will be soaking wet and I'll look like I've been to the Vietnam War. I don't look great at those moments. Even the fresh T-shirt will be wet because after that level of exertion, you keep sweating for ages. I shower, get back into my normal clothes, throw the wet stuff into the washing machine and do a wash. By then I'll be fucked and every muscle in my body will be throbbing, revolting, protesting against the way it's been abused. That is a great feeling."

Helen Kaye, a serial dope smoker, likes skanking at gigs, jumping around real fast while joyously lifting her knees up high. She is a good-looking teenager given to mohawks and fucked-up denim. Her parents are academics but Helen refused to go to university. She gets heavily involved with the global anti-capitalist movement, and regularly treks off to Seattle or New York to protest against the World Bank. She lives with her boyfriend who works for a small record label:

"One of the things I do is I organise strategy for rioters. I guess you could say I'm involved in the paramilitary end of the anti-capitalist movement! There are ways of dealing with cops in riots, and it's my job to work out those methodologies. I do these rather surreal computer projections, making use of street maps of places where we may be planning a march, demo, riot. Whatever the fuck you want to call it. It comes as no surprise, then, to find that I get more out of moshing than most. Let the chaos descend

and let me have a good look! Not that I'm standing there like an asshole watching how it goes. I get stuck in, that's actually my advantage. I know what chaos is really like. Take my word, there are people – cops, corporations – who are taping and watching moshing with a cold analytical eye, seeking to extend their control over folks.

"Right now people are bug-eyed about moshing. In music it has kind of replaced Marilyn Manson as media public enemy number one. I totally agree with all these protests against attacks on women in the pit but bad attitudes towards women exist all over society and are being sold by the large corporations. Not a lot is being done about sexism in everyday life.

"It comes as no surprise to find that Fred Durst of Limp Bizkit, who is such a total misogynist, is also an executive at Interscope Records. Sex sells. I have been groped in the pit by assholes but I've been visually raped or groped or otherwise downpressed all over this society of ours. Don't blame it on the pit. I've been moshing since I was thirteen and I hope to do it 'til I drop. I love to go where there are insane people doing their best to survive. I like to stand my ground like a motherfucker, to roll with the punches while defending myself. I think I'm pretty good at doing a good circle kick which seems to keep me safe. That means I use one foot to go around in a circle while, with the other foot, I'm kicking out.

"When I started off I thought I was great, that I really had the skills down. Now of course I see kids making their way into the pit those first times and they look so confident. They remind me of my stupid younger self. The thing I hate the most is the people who come up behind you when you're on the edge of the pit and shove you in, whether you're full-on moshing or not. They're just ultra-straight jerks treating you like you're the very freak they've read all about in the papers. I also hate the guys who feel real inadequate in life so they feel they must come on like tough guys in the pit.

"*This happens the most when you're at school because you're hanging around in small circles. When I was at high school all the 'responsible punks' used to organise an annual gig in the Community Centre which was really a mosh party. We all had to pay $3 and bring a can of refried beans or something – it was a benefit for the homeless. There were local cops hanging around outside and certain parents – the cool ones – would be present to act as chaperones. You'd be there with a furrowed brow moshing – hating everyone – and all the other jerks from your school would be there, everybody watching everybody else like a hawk. We had to take all our drugs before we got there. The 'responsible punks' had agreed that there'd be no drugs or drink. It was a total joke. Well, at shows like that, you'd see the inadequate guys, the guys who'd bought the wrong album and the wrong trainers, doing their tough guy routine.*

"*One of the best things about moshing in the US, I don't know how it goes in Europe or elsewhere, is the multiracial nature of it. A lot of bands like Madball and Marauder have Latinos in the line-up, and you notice quite a lot of blacks in the pit too. Not enough. Moshing is moving on for sure. I think a lot of the small scene people – the people on my scene – are disillusioned with it. The pit remains a great way to work out all the shit that's going on in your life. Or to work it out of your system. Violence is good for you in the right atmosphere, just so long as you're in love with the whole experience, not just with the violence. You got to catch the people you see falling. You got to watch out for yourself, avoid feet that may be flying in your direction. You've got to stay focused on where you are, enjoy the music, enjoy the privilege of participating in the music.*"

Sepultura/Soulfly

In the early days after the Sepultura split, it looked like Max Cavalera had the big momentum and that the new Max-less Sepultura would be the losers. Cavalera quit the band amid confusion and a flurry of acrimony, his emotions seemingly blurred by the '96 murder of his stepson Dana Wells in what was allegedly a crack connected car crash near the Cavalera home in Phoenix. On the day that Wells died, Cavalera was out on the road with Sepultura. When he arrived at the Donnington Festival site in England, where the band were due to play, Sepultura guitarist Andreas Kisser broke the bad news to Cavalera and his wife Gloria, Sepultura's manager at the time. Ozzy Osbourne, who was also playing Donnington, loaned the Cavaleras his private jet so they could get home right away.

There followed an odd period of reflection on Cavalera's part, creating a distance between himself and the band that he, with his brother and buddies, had formed in Brazil back in the mid-Eighties. During that dark time of mourning Cavalera put together his new project, Soulfly, which was supposed to take on board various current developments such as the infusion of rock with hip-hop-related beats and the trimmed down nature of the new more intelligent style in metal. These changes were in danger of turning the likes of Slayer, Pantera, and Sepultura into downright dinosaurs.

172

The other guys in Sepultura – including Max's drummer brother Igor – were entitled to be outraged by Cavalera's departure. At that moment in time they were riding the crest of a wave. With combined album sales of 5,000,000 and the critically acclaimed gold album *Roots* under their collective belt, it very much looked as if Sepultura were about to go into orbit.

The first eponymous Soulfly album came wrapped up in grief to do with the death of Dana Wells, a dreadlocked provincial druggie who'd lead a life peripheral to the rock monster that Sepultura had become. He'd co-written 'Attitude' on *Roots*, liked to stage dive to The Deftones and Sepultura, wore piercings on his face. He had his own street wear clothing company in California, worked in the Sepultura office, and intended doing a little freelance talent scouting/A&R work. According to Gloria Cavalera the pals who were with him when he died were "groupies, Sepultura groupies, and therefore Dana groupies."

The golden age of Sepultura had been a good time for music. With Cavalera's departure an important experiment in metal seemed to come crashing to the ground. *Roots* differed from the band's thrash metal origins, and from the ongoing output of their contemporaries, in a very fundamental way. It spurted and shook with feral tunes, rhythm, and an unadulterated melodic sense. *Roots* was Sepultura's way of saying that they were no longer a jobbing metal crew. They were a mature proposition complete with their own ideas about, for instance, the relationship between the so-called Third World and the First. *Roots* held out a lifeline to Sepultura, suggesting that at a time when their generation of bands were developing a touch of rigor mortis, the Brazilians were rebelling against that. The straitjacket that goes hand in hand with longevity was rejected; they forged themselves a defiant new identity.

There was nothing quite like the Sepultura live show at that time. Combining the ballsy assault of their earlier work with the cadences of raw Brazilian percussion, they were on to a winner. I saw Sepultura twice in their last years. It was while moshing in pits driven by Sepultura that I first convinced myself that moshing was both a legitimate and valuable experience. They were one of those special bands who got extra brownie points; they could turn a whole venue into a pit. They punched the air with singular assurance. Kids and older fans bounced as one on the floor, dancing and laughing and moving like wild dervishes. To be in the Sepultura pit was to be possessed by a near-erotic sense of freedom in music. The tribal nature of their new sound created a very real tribe out there on the dancefloor. Tough players in the rock game, from a tough part of the world, late Nineties Sepultura was a unique proposition. They seemed unassailable.

Or, rather, they were externally unassailable. The enemy within is always the worst enemy. Cavalera proved very smart in his Soulfly strategy. It was astute to take the hip-hop thing on board, and also to use his iconic status to rub up against hot newcomers like Fred Durst and Chino Moreno. It was also wise of him to make a generational leap by ditching his mid-thirties Brazilian pals and replacing them with hip young gunslingers who enjoyed session player status in Soulfly.

Grafting these youthful players onto the percussive innovations first displayed on *Roots,* Cavalera and Soulfly made a serious attempt to pick up where Sepultura had left off. When I spoke to Cavalera he went on at length about the way he wanted the percussion to go.

> *"There are no boundaries to where the music will take me now. I want to take that side of Soulfly which is based on the beat and go with it. I don't see this stopping with Brazilian drumming. I want to expand the number of drummers we have onstage and I want to take in diverse percussive influences. I want to take on*

board African drumming in particular . . . I think it's important that Soulfly make a statement about the unity of peoples."

From the word go Soulfly were thinking big. It would be fair to say that Cavalera worked himself up into quite a rhetorical state, seeing himself as an heroic Bob Marley-style Third World leader and visionary. The whole of South America and exploited peoples all over the world had been uplifted by the Sepultura success story. Taking this positive image on board, Cavalera saw himself as leading something more than a metal band. He was now at the head of a movement which was very vague but potentially powerful.

"When we were in the studio doing the Soulfly album, the idea was to collaborate with a lot of people and make it like a rap type of ideology with people dropping in on every song. Chino from The Deftones was one of them, as Fred (Durst) was one of them . . . I had this killer song 'Bleed'. . . Fred met with me and I was like this is some serious heavy shit. It's about my really close friend being murdered. I'd like you to rap on it but keep the spirit. I left the vocal booth and Ross (Robinson, producer of Slipknot, Limp Bizkit, At The Drive-In) said walk around and let us do our thing and then come back and listen. I stayed outside the studio for about two hours and when I came back it was awesome."

I first saw Soulfly in '98 with Limp Bizkit in support. There was loads of hip interface, not the least of this hipness being the manner in which Cavalera dragged Limp Bizkit, already the boys most likely to succeed; around on the road like symbolic proof of his own freshness and youthful vigour. He took every opportunity to rub up against Durst's strong presence and youth appeal. Durst came onstage with them every night to sing 'Bleed'. "Fred used to come out," Cavalera recalled, "wearing only a sock, a fucked-up looking sock that you could see through. I was tripped out sometimes and I'd be like,

'Man, you scared me right now', but it was cool."

It was cool for Soulfly in particular, as Max Cavalera quick marched away from Sepultura's 15 years of achievement and heritage. It was obvious, via their Korn and Limp Bizkit connections, that Limp Bizkit were happening. Soulfly cleverly hitched themselves to a rising star. Nevertheless, Cavalera insisted that he was unaware of Bizkit's status.

> *"I don't know if I thought they'd be as big a band as they've become, but they had a lot of hunger. They were serious about what they were doing. The music with the hip hop had a different aspect that could reach a lot of people."*

On the '98 show that I caught, Limp Bizkit played a remarkably weak set in front of a crowd who, in part, had come to see them. Their crowd manipulation – which would subsequently garner them the mainstream headlines that every band covets – was very much in evidence but so, too, was the vacuous nature of their white boy read on hip hop.

In the pit during Soulfly it was like old times. I spent the entire night in a place where there was an amazing level of carnival dancing performed by dreadlocked men, lots of punky singing, and general whooping about. There was a spirit of rebellion and rapport reminiscent of long forgotten Bob Marley concerts; it seemed that Max Cavalera was going to achieve effortlessly his right-on global agenda.

When Sepultura finally got over the Cavalera defection, they made a decision which shocked the industry; they decided to keep on going. The general idea in the music business is that when the lead guy quits a band, the rest of them are supposed to fuck off and die. But Sepultura were rugged individuals. While their past gave them some old baggage, it also gave them a platform. A lot of people were heavily into their message. They recruited a new singer, a powerful black American hardcore vocalist called Derek Green, and they angrily flung a new album – *Against* – into the marketplace. Andreas Kisser, who now became the effective leader of the band, told me that it was a traumatic time for them. "We didn't just lose our lead singer. We also lost our manager. So it was a very confused time for us. It took us quite a while to get over that and to settle down into being a band again. *Against* was recorded in the middle of that whole thing."

It is the nature of metal journalists, who work within the industry, to tow the party line and to acclaim new product from important bands on important labels. *Against* was well received, and the new Sepultura went on tour as the half of an intriguing double bill with Slayer, who'd created their own vision of intelligent white noise under the stewardship of producer Rick Rubin. Subsequently, with the benefit of about six month's hindsight, the media deemed *Against* a confused disappointment. Sepultura, when I caught them with Slayer, delivered the goods.

Their drawing power was undoubtedly down since the split. While I'd seen Cavalera headline a five thousand seater, Sepultura were doing the opening slot to Slayer in a hall less than half that size. This didn't seem to bother them as they whacked out a slice of noise which blended in very well with Slayer's timeless assault. Sepultura came well out of the competition. A Brazilian who'd followed them for five years reckoned that they had the potential to survive.

"When you have guys like this who've worked together for so long you have a real energy resource. You're seeing a band who almost have a life of their own. They will never be defeated by the fact that Max is gone. Hey, he has his own thing to do. I really liked it. I danced the whole night through with Soulfly. He was a good new sound for himself, I'm proud of him. I had such a good time that I must have been giving off a good vibe because I met this beautiful woman who came back to my place with me so . . . hey

. . . I don't pick up any woman here tonight. This is a man's night. I think I got higher on the sound of the new Sepultura than I did with Soulfly. My head is really buzzing from the sound and from the dancing. I smoked a load of grass before I came here but the noise has just been making me higher and higher."

I reached New York's Hammerstein Ballroom late and Soulfly were already onstage when I entered the hall. There must have been four thousand people with their backs to me, staring at a far away stage where Soulfly were thrashing away. From the back of the hall the sound was thin so I made my way through the crowd as quickly as I could, ducking and diving between small enclaves of fanatical Pantera fans who didn't want to let me pass. By far and away the largest number of people were there to catch Pantera – a running joke as far as I was concerned – and they were huddled in little groups talking or enjoying the music without paying all that much attention to it. They were a porcine looking crew of dumbos. It was ironic to see Soulfly, whose stance demanded one's full attention, playing to the unconverted. Since Pantera are infamous for lengthy guitar solos that make Eric Clapton look economical and with-it, it was hardly surprising that their fans found all this hip-hop shit a walk too far on the wild side. There were small moshing ghettoes scattered here and there. I was alarmed, for just a moment, when I stumbled into one pit containing a number of active burly moshers wearing pulled down balaclavas.

Village Voice commented two days earlier on the irony of Soulfly and Sepultura both playing New York in the same week, Soulfly doing two nights supporting Pantera at the Hammerstein while Sepultura were headlining the smaller Irving Plaza in between doing a couple of out of town headliners. *Village Voice* suggested that the two Cavalera brothers should mend their fences and get the *Roots*-epoch Sepultura back together.

In the three years since they'd formed, Soulfly had suffered a seemingly endless series of line-up changes. Although they initially enjoyed big momentum, most people still wanted to see the old team glued back together again. This seemed profoundly unlikely given that both parties were still refusing to speak to one another.

The average age of the crowd declined as I made my way through them. The front of stage has a reasonable pit made up of the youngest people in the hall. They didn't in any way look like metal heads, more like the ambitious rainbow coalition constituency that Cavalera had set out to capture. Latino punks, blond blue-eyed dreadlocked youths, black guys in leather, funny little girls with loads of attitude. The band sounded almost as quiet up front as they had from the back of the hall. By the time I eventually reached the stage they were leaving to cheerful roars from the front and polite clapping from everywhere else. Such is the fate of support bands, no matter how important they seem.

The usual changeovers in the pit began as equipment changeovers proceeded onstage. The kids fled. Given the difference between the Soulfly/Sepultura agenda and the rather bovine approach of Pantera, I wasn't surprised to see many of them gathered outside the Hammerstein when I quit the scene myself about an hour later, twenty minutes into Pantera.

Three days later about 500 shabby looking men and women huddled against the wind and the rain outside the Irving Plaza, located in a swish student part of town, normally the venue for student-friendly shows. Lee Strasberg's acting school – home to aspirant Brandos and Pacinos – is located right around the corner. The mid-twenties crowd gathered to hear Sepultura looked a bit out of place. They were largely South American, the South Americans were mainly poor looking Brazilians, and the rest of the queue was made up of slightly older prosperous white folk – leftovers from the commercial harvest reaped after *Roots* – and some dubious looking Nineties metallers.

Sepultura were promoting their second post-Max album, *Nation*. Andreas Kisser told me that the band were seeking with *Nation* to create, and speak for, "a world without borders or religion. A world where ecology is important. I feel we have a powerful message for the nation which is Sepultura and their fans. An underground cosmos of solidarity."

Irving Plaza was sold out and the pride these people took in their band was palpable. Most of those I spoke to had yet to hear the new line-up and were interested to hear my report on what they'd been like with Slayer. They spoke frankly of their expectations from the night. One woman said she was sure they'd not be as good as the Max-led version. Her husband got all humpy at this, as loyal to his band as he probably was to his soccer team. He was wearing the yellow jersey of the Brazilian team.

Inside the atmosphere was mellow and subdued until the bands started. The support acts more or less blew Sepultura off. Vision Of Disorder and Hatebreed performed with all the energy they could muster, both bands employing tactics right out of rap and hip hop, both coming on like angry posses looking for trouble. The crowd were wowed out by their bravura displays of testosterone-rich intensity and it was diffi-cult to see how Sepultura could top these thick slices of fury which appealed to pits which were street-gang orientated, their gear entirely derived from various hip-hop styles. The people on the stage were singing their song. There was lots of very rough dancing. When I got home that night I found three large purple bruises on my torso.

Before Sepultura strode on, a pre-recorded message from the Irving Plaza authorities warned us that, even though moshing was barred in the venue, there would undoubtedly be moshing during the forthcoming set. Those of us who wished to avoid this moshing should leave the pit right away. The Irving Plaza were in no way responsible . . . blah, blah, blah. This sounded fine by me. Given the intensity of what I'd already seen, and the fun I'd always had in Sepultura pits, the warning led me to believe that all hell was about to break loose. But moshing during the support slots had been so very intense that when Sepultura came on to a hero's welcome, the crowd was sticky but exhausted.

Sepultura's decision to do a defiant set based around new stuff from *Nation* that the crowd didn't know – eight songs from an album not yet released – was brave but odd. After the first three or four tunes there was no moshing at all. The crowd stood perfectly still for the bulk of the night, forcing themselves to applaud vigorously between songs. There was great loyalty going out to the band but there was no getting around the fact that Sepultura without moshing (and Max Cavalera by implication) was an utter disaster. People were continually asking one another what they thought of the new stuff and the band. Everyone was agreeing that it was all very good. Very good band. Very good songs. Great frontman. Just that they didn't seem to be enjoying it too much. And there was no moshing.

For their impressive loyalty the fans were rewarded towards the end with a few golden oldies. This raised their spirits and sent them home sweating. *Kerrang* in a review of the gig noted the crowd's dimming enthusiasm for the new material but concluded that "the challenge, at least for tonight, is met". I wasn't so convinced, though I wish I was. *Nation* was a good album – it deserved the oxygen of success – but I reckoned Sepultura had a problem. Good metal now exists within the confines of a hip-hop universe. If you're not hip to that, you're not hip to the pit, and if you're not hip to the pit, you have a big fight on your hands.

Outside afterwards it was still wet and cold. I overheard

three or four separate conversations about how Derek Green
was a good frontman but no replacement for Max Cavalera. A
20-year-old Brazilian – Tiago – that I'd hooked up with in
Hatebreed's pit started talking to me. I'd noticed him not too
far away during the Sepultura set, staring intensely at the
various band members. Tiago had enjoyed it very much,
thought it was a new band with a wide-open road in front of it.
But he missed the pits from the old days.

> *"I guess some of it could be because I was younger back in those*
> *days. I felt good with myself. They was my band. I'd go to see*
> *them with my homies, or we'd listen to tapes of their shit in my*
> *room. I thought they'd be around forever like they existed then,*
> *kind of fucking following up* Roots *with* Roots II *and then* Son
> of Roots . . . *which was just me being a stupid jerk I guess.*
> *Anyway they fucked up and that fucked it up for a lot of people*
> *like me . . . we became grown up when Max quit. It was like a*
> *death in the family. I think it's great that Sepultura are still out*
> *there and the new singer is a good one. Sepultura created the*
> *fucking Sepulnation, you know? This ectopic universe where we*
> *all exist as equals. You got to stick with your own people through*
> *good days and bad days."*

Hardcore Soft Porn – Sex In The Pit

AD Rock from The Beastie Boys once announced that their next tour would feature a "tough guy pit, the hippy peace pit, and the orgy pit." Kid Rock sings about getting into the pit and trying to love someone. Mick Thomson, the guitarist with Slipknot, says that, "If there wasn't such a thing as masturbation there'd definitely be a body count."

At the age when most people come to moshing, the experience is part and parcel of their sexual awakening. Their willingness to accept the risks involved is symptomatic of the same complex period in their lives. D.P. Weinberger, who works at the Clinical Brain Disorders Laboratory in the US's National Institute of Health wrote in the *New York Times*:

> *The evidence is unequivocal that the prefrontal cortex of a fifteen-year-old is biologically immature. The connections are not final, the networks are still being strengthened, and the full capacity for inhibitory control in still years away. The 15-year-old brain does not have the biological machinery to inhibit impulses in the service of long term planning.*

Suzanne, a funky looking woman in her early twenties, works in a rare bookshop in San Francisco. She used to wear a lot of restyled workwear but now that she is that little bit older she tends towards black suits which give her a vaguely Goth look. She styles herself a radical feminist and says with a full throated laugh that, for the seven months she spent moshing, she was a "wanton wench".

> *"I was sixteen so I was entirely focused on screwing. I wasn't an actual virgin but I felt like one . . . specially the night after I lost my virginity!! I was – still am – into hardcore. All my pals were into Madonna and shit and they regarded me as being pretty much out on a limb. I had this one pal Lisa who used to go to the gigs with me. There would be these scary looking guys with big broad shoulders and flared nostrils. This used to turn the two of us really on. We were so young at the time that they all seemed incredibly mature and old. In fact a lot of them weren't much more than a year older than us. I'd go to maybe six gigs a month and Lisa to, let's say, maybe four. The minute the lights went out I was busy. I think it was up to the girls to make the first moves. You know . . . letting your hand drift accidentally across some guy's crotch. If he seemed to like it, as when he smiled back at you, you took it from there. I'd say I scored that way at least twice a month. The guys had cars or places of their own. Or they knew a friend or older brother who had a room we could go back to. I think I became a little addicted to this easy access to sex. The last time I left the mosh pit, eight years ago, I looked back wistfully as I walked away. It was like returning home after a fantastic voyage when you're a child. I remember I said to myself, 'Well, girl, you'll never be here again.' And I never did go back. The sex clarified my mind. I had such a good introduction to sex free from possessiveness and all that."*

The mosh pit operates as a counterculture nightclub allowing participants to get to know one another intimately amid the darkness, the flashing lights, and the noise. Dr. Joan Camper from the Getliffe Institute in Los Angeles, a psychologist who has made a study of sexuality in the pits of California, told me that it only stands to reason.

"You have these kids worked up to a really frantic level at a time in their lives when they're coming to terms with their own sexuality. Believe me I know all about it. My son was a fan of Soundgarden and Nirvana many years ago. I used to pick him up after gigs and he'd be in excelcis. These children spend an hour letting out all this energy into the atmosphere and touching up against each other in that heat and sweat. As with any nightclub scenario, naturally, most of the action takes place afterwards. Given the age of the kids involved, mid-teens to twenties, most of this sex would happen up some back alley near the venue or in some park or discreet public space. They're not yet of an age where they'll have places of their own. This is no big deal, just your average rites of passage stuff. What goes on in the pit is a different matter. Obviously there's loads of groping. You can hardly avoid groping or being groped, it happens anyway as a result of random touching.

"To be crude about it, there are quite a few hand jobs. You could get a hand job discreetly in the melee. Full-on penetrative sex is rare enough. We're talking about kids and they're self-conscious about any kind of sexual exhibitionism. When you have an older crowd, who have a bit of experience, you find occasional brave souls willing to throw caution to the wind and do it on the spot. But that would only happen at the more extreme shows. Homosexuality? This is controversial. Heterosexual commentators say it's virtually non-existent. Gays say there's quite a bit of it. What can I say? The 'accusation' of homosexuality is one regularly flung at moshers, what with the bronzed torsos, all that sweaty embracing. Participants in the pit can be touchy on the topic. There is this website www.moshersaregay.com. *Don't ask me."*

Bergin looks like a young Kris Kristoffersen, complete with a Texas drawl and torn blue denims. He rattles on a lot with his opinions and takes it all very seriously. He says that the bands he likes are "curious about the future and bored by the past."

185

He has lots of catch phrases like that but I feel he picked them up in magazine reviews rather than made them up himself. This is not to say that his comments are irrelevant.

"I think one of the things which makes the pit such a sexy place is the almost total absence of posturing and affectation there. You meet one another on a level playing field and there is no dishonesty. You're in trouble or on the ropes all the time so you don't have the time to be worried about looking cool. A girl is looking at you and she sees you fucked up, tired, sweating. She looks and feels even worse. What you see is what you get. There tends to be few couples there. Girls in the pit tend to be alone, along with the guys. Therefore there is little cause for rivalry or possessiveness since no one gets left out. And the restraints – the peer restraints – that normally moderate your behaviour are gone with the wind.

"The first time I saw actual sex in the pit was at Revolting Cocks sometime in the early Nineties. I was 17 at the time and it made a big impression on me. I'd been waiting for months to see the Cocks. I was all worked up over them. They had these great tracks like this filthy vile rewrite of Rod Stewart's 'Do Ya Think I'm Sexy'. And that big dancefloor hit of theirs was on the boil at that moment I think. 'Beers And Steers And Queers'. Those guys had a total sexual agenda. I noticed this beautiful looking lady standing on the very edge of the pit which was pretty fucking crazy that night. With the Cocks it was music for dancing to anyway and there were a number of clubbing people mixed in there with the industrial and rock gangs. The club crowd are horny anyway. That's why they go to their fucking clubs. This woman I'm talking about looked like real club people. She was dressed to the nines in expensive designer clothes. She had on an almost luminous red business suit and some cool looking jewellery; she looked like a banker or attorney. She stood completely out because everybody else was freaky looking. There were loads of girls there but they were mainly in bondage sort of gear or punk

gear or rockist. Some girls that I really liked and if I'd been man enough . . . There was this total dirtbag moshing like a motherfucker. He was a small little fellow but well built. All he had on was a pair of combats so you could see his impressive physique. He started sort of dancing in front of this well dressed lady in the suit. She was tall so he could scope her from far away and he was totally scoping her!! They were neither of them all that young. She was around thirty and he was maybe a little younger, looking good for their age. I had him down as the world's biggest loser. He looked like dirt. But she looked randy enough and, eventually, on for it. She moved maybe six feet forward and he made this big leap at her. Like Tarzan leaping from tree to tree. Next thing you know he was literally wrapped around her. He was . . . legs and arms . . . wrapped around her like a little chimpanzee. Don't ask me how they managed it in terms of clothes. It was easy enough for him I suppose, and she was wearing a dress, but maybe ten minutes later they were fucking right there in the middle of the pit. I don't know to what extent people were aware of what was happening but I sure was. This was the first time I ever actually saw two people having sex. Now that I think about it, it was the last time too."

Larry is a tall muscular Scottish skinhead with a long blond goatee. I met him with his boyfriend in an Atari Teenage Riot pit. He was wearing a Queer Nation T-shirt, FUBU jeans, and black Vans trainers. His boyfriend, an unfriendly American teenager who looked like he played in a Ramones tribute band, distressed denim and everything, kept telling Larry not to talk to me because I was a "fucker". But Larry was a mellow dude, and he found his pal's ratty attitude funny. I think he wanted to talk to me about his experiences because he felt that people might benefit from hearing his story.

"I fell in love in the pit. I was this good-looking blond blue-eyed lad. I had very long curly blond hair, my pride and joy that I'd

been working on for three years. I moved down to London from
Scotland in '98. I was 17 and I'd been fixed up with a job by my
cousin, who worked in a South London pub. I shared a room
over the pub with the cousin. He was good enough to me but it
was like living in a wardrobe with someone. We'd been good
mates back when I was 11 or 12 but that was a long forgotten
time in my life when I reached town. I'd had a few boyfriends
back home just before I left but I made it difficult for myself by not
being interested in clubs or cruising. I think my taste in men grew
out of my interest in metal. My favourite bands were Slayer, Iron
Maiden, and Sepultura. I guess you could say that I've learned a
few things since then! I was into this metal fantasy of big, tall
rock dudes with long, long hair. All I can say in my own defence
is that it was more or less funny, if not pathetic.

"I felt very confined. I worked and I hung out in my room.
Anyway the next thing was that Sepultura were doing a gig so I
had to go. I'd had a few drinks and a smoke beforehand. Between
the darkness and the booze I was that bit looser. So off I went
down the front where all the sexy guys were. The next hour I had
the time of my life slapping up against all these friendly men
though I was very cautious. You know the way they go on about
the homoerotic homophobic mosh pit. They were happy enough
about a little sweat touching sweat but I don't think they'd have
been too happy about it going any further. Then I was looking at
this dude and he was looking at me. He was not the type I had in
mind but he looked great. In his early twenties. His torso was
covered with tattoos. His arms had tattoos of branches and vines
while his back was dominated by this large abstract blood-red orb.
We worked our way closer to one another which meant backing
out of where we were, where it was pretty tight and clammy. We
moved back a yard or two to where it was more like dancing than
moshing. I said to him, 'You do know that I'm a guy, don't
you?' because I found it too good to be true that he was interested.
He had this kind of twangy American accent and he laughed,

'*Of course I know you're a fucking guy, Man.*' *We went to the Men's Room where we stayed in a cubicle until two bouncers cleared us out about after the encores. They fixed us with these filthy looks even though I think they thought we were doing drugs rather than . . . My hero fucked off pretty quick and refused to give me his number. I was a bit pissed off. Next time I saw him, about a year and a half later, I was a hardened criminal. I think it was at Soulfly and the funny thing was that I was almost looking out for him, expecting him to show up.*"

Bastard Sons Of JFK – Dropkick Murphys

The fat rights movement in America is campaigning to have the word "fat" ruled an offensive term similar to "nigger" and "queer". They're campaigning to have two seats each when they get on planes and other important civil liberties issues. Dropkick Murphys' St Patrick's Eve party at New York's Wetlands looked a bit like the Annual Convention of the Fat Party.

The Dropkick Murphys have been slogging away at their Irish hardcore since '96. Their success had been remorselessly slow but sure. When I caught up with them at Wetlands their most recent album, *Sing Loud Sing Proud* on the cool-defining Epitaph label, was breaking down big barriers for them. One reason for this was that *Sing Loud* featured a few cameo appearances by Shane MacGowan whose critical reputation remains intact in New York. This gave them a critical cachet they'd previously lacked as a common or garden vein-bursting hardcore lynch mob. Their none-too-subtle press campaign seemed to imply that a baton of some sort had been passed on from MacGowan, a spent force, to them. As luck would have it, the real thing was doing a handful of gigs in New York that very weekend. There were rumours that MacGowan might join the Dropkicks on stage, but it was as well for them that he didn't. When you've seen the best, you're looking at the rest.

I'd seen the Dropkicks a few times previously and – but for their name – I'd noticed little by way of an Irish interface.

They were fat-headed family men lead by a chap called Al Barr, they rocked the joint, moved the pit, did their job. I'd caught them in the middle of a plethora of new punk tours that passed through Europe in '98 and '99. So many punk-lite and generic hardcore acts erupted out of the US B-Division in the aftermath of the Green Day and The Offspring chart triumphs that, while they all drew crowds and provided the backdrop for some silly pits, few stood out in hindsight. One of the things I remembered about the Dropkicks was that they did too many cover versions, not normally a sign that you've seen the future of rock'n'roll and it works.

The Dropkicks were making big moves to ensure a steady niche for themselves on the circuit. They added a bagpipes player called Spicey McHaggis and a mandolin/tin whistle player by the name of Foltz to their line-up. Wrapping the green flag firmly round themselves, their set now featured 'The Rocky Road To Dublin' and 'The Irish Rover', in addition to new tunes, 'The Fortunes Of War' and 'Heroes From Our Past' that sounded – very vaguely – like political ballads. A review of *Sing Loud Sing Proud* in the Irish rock paper, *Hot Press*, compared them to Sham 69 without the songs, the worst thrash metal band you've ever heard, and the infantile macho posturings of American wrestling. The Dropkicks, it said, represented "an Ireland that only exists in the USA."

Things are nevertheless going good for them. Guys from Boston wearing leprechaun tattoos they may be, but they've been featured on the soundtrack to *The Sopranos,* and there was slam dancing at Tower Records when they did an acoustic set there.

Dropkick Murphys was the name of a rough and ready drying-out dive for Irish alcoholics in Boston in the Thirties. They used to physically tie their clients down and leave them there until they'd fought their addiction.

As I queued to get in I had no idea what awaited me. Most of the people in the queue looked pretty civilised and collegiate. When I started getting pestered by demented Japanese fans with dyed hair who were offering big bucks for my ticket I remembered the trendoid angle on the gig. Lars Fredericksen, guitarist with punkier-than-thou Rancid, had produced two albums by the Dropkicks. He was in town with them to do a slot supporting a new album by his solo project, Lars Fredericksen and The Bastards. This explained the reasonably civilised tone of the queue. I'd been prepared for a bunch of drunken punk louts or even drunker Irish American louts. Unbeknownst to me the biggest number of seriously fat Irish Americans I'd ever see in one place at one time were already inside Wetlands, waiting to strike.

I was queuing for the second Dropkicks show that night. They were heading back to their native Boston the following morning, due to do two St Patrick's Day shows when they got to their hometown. Fredericksen hadn't played at the earlier Wetlands show and was not travelling on to Boston. Rancid sell truckloads of records to a lot of middle-class kids and this showed on that rainy night as tickets changed hands for $75 and $100. The people who tended to sell their tickets were the poorer looking ones and those who'd come because they wanted to celebrate St Patrick's Day from the word go. Those buying the tickets were either eccentric looking Japanese – some of them more or less transvestites – or very rich student punks with all the right skateboard gear.

Once inside Wetlands the overriding atmosphere was con-genial American Irish. If you're Irish come into the parlour. The air was full of loud references to Ireland, Dublin, Shane MacGowan, Clinton, Guinness. Stiff Little Fingers, The Under-tones and The Pogues were the main items on the turntables. It was hard to move around the club, a nicely designed small space crowded with punks there to catch the Rancid prime mover, a lot of politically dubious looking skinheads, and a slew of grotesque mammoths of obvious Irish extraction let out for the night to catch the Dropkicks. There are some thin Irish Americans too. You could tell the Irish by their Irish T-shirts, peaked caps with lime green shamrock insignia, and other cultural phenomena of that sort which you'd never expect to encounter at a hardcore show. A quick visit to the Dropkick's busy merchandise stall revealed embossed key rings, pint glasses, and one-shot spirits glasses. I had never seen such merchandise.

The thin Irish sported Clancy Brothers-style Donegal Tweed peaked caps, white jumpers, and white chinos. They looked stupid in their clothes but they were smart enough individuals and well capable of looking after themselves. The mammoths all looked like bastard sons of John F. Kennedy. Each and every one of them had that sort of Irish American muttonhead you associate with Charles During, most of the Kennedys, and Tip O'Neill. Their heads were their finest features. Below non-existent necks they swelled out to elephantine dimensions. They were dressed in white trash casuals. Synthetic open necked shirts and stay-pressed grey slacks, white synthetic brogues. The occasional green or white cardigan, jumper, or jacket was also in evidence but it was blistering hot in Wetlands so most of that stuff must've been in the cloakroom. The fat boys made some odd facial gestures and had strange notions about interacting with the rest of us. You'd have been forgiven for thinking that the whole lot of them had been let out of the funny farm for the day.

Closer to the small stage were all the pretty punk girls and boys who'd come to see the Rancid guitarist. They had that whole area to themselves and their excitement was as intense as anything you'd encounter at a big-time gig or festival. Keeping their distance from the kids, but mingling towards the back with the Irish, were a variety of uptight-looking and very drunk rednecks who, for some reason, had a decidedly right-wing look about them. I guess it was those looks of withering contempt they were laying on the punks.

It seems that fascists have been drawn to the Dropkicks because of their singalongapunk style, the blue collar aspirational nature of their lyrics, and the heavy male drinking which is part of their image. A number of the people around me had the distinct look of men who'd done time. Some of them were wearing nice looking combat trousers but many more sported indifferent blue jeans.

"It is an odd thing to have Nazis at shows coming over and being like 'I love you man!'," Al Barr once said disingenuously. "There's nothing we can do about who listens to us, so there's no point getting pissed off."

There are, of course, all manner of things that bands can do about ridding themselves of fascist followers. Many punk acts have self-inflicted damage on their careers in order to enjoy the luxury of not playing to fascists. The Dropkicks claim not to be in any sense fascist, and profess a progressive political agenda. Nevertheless their workerist celebration of "working-class solidarity, friendship, loyalty, and self-improvement as a means to bettering society" (like it says on their website) is open to many interpretations. Especially when they believe that "If you pick yourself up by the bootstraps and live your life to the best of your ability you may set an example that others will follow. The power of your example is far greater than what you say."

Fredericksen has this relationship with the Dropkicks which predates their complete conversion to folk-rock, a genre referred to in Ireland as Sham Rock. I couldn't help but feel that Fredericksen and his fans were not exactly in the right place at the right time. Nevertheless he came on stage like a real trooper and did a fun set, way more innovative and truly punk than Rancid's Clash-by-numbers methodology. Fredericksen had enough upbeat self-confidence to command the stage. The Bastards, complete with a balaclava-wearing vocalist, were acutely suited to his street punk anthems.

His fans got good value for money. The various mutton-heads left the pit to the punks who had a very light-hearted kiddy mosh made up of old-style punk pogoing with some very modest crowd surfing. The fat Irish guys loomed around the edges of the pit, fondling pint glasses of beer, none of them seeming to know one another. They stared straight ahead, betrayed no emotion, profoundly indifferent to Fredericksen's brilliant efforts. The big boys were busy waiting. From time to time one of them would sneak a resentful look at the punks bouncing effortlessly around a loosely full dancefloor.

The inevitable transition which followed Fredericksen's encore was peaceful. It's always nice to catch an arena filler playing in a bar, so the punks got an adult portion show. Many of them were heading for the exit and the others, all too aware of the Attack of The Killer Tellytubbies that was looming up behind them, ceded the space. One by one the big guys moved in for their heroes. By the time the Dropkicks hit the stage half an hour later, all those guys were rammed in there, plus a load of fascist tough guys, some Blacks, and a number of very tough looking women in black leather jackets, etc. Chants of "Lets Go Murphys" hammered the air for ten minutes before they came on.

By then I was getting used to the brutality of the New York pits. The New York hardcore scene wrote the book on pit bar-barism a long time ago. The second the Dropkicks played their first note the fat Irish started moving erratically and somewhat disturbingly in the direction of the stage. It was like they were all having epileptic fits at the same time. If they'd been thin and able to move around a bit more it probably would have looked more like pogoing. As it happened it looked like wobbling. They wobbled effectively over the Drop-kick's raw Oi punk rants fuelled by some energetic military snare work. When they got a good feel for the sound the fatties floated around the pit hitting off of everything in sight like malevolent billiard balls. They were big and resistant so they could view all opposition with a mutt-like calm.

This calm was not reflected in the behaviour of the other elements in the pit. The skinheads were organised customers despite their abject drunkenness. A smattering of the black guys present were insinuating themselves into an already tight situation. The skinheads and the Irish were inclined to ignore the blacks, pretending they didn't exist, but, it being the pit, all and sundry ended up in very close contact. As so very often, the pit was yet again reflective of life itself.

When the Dropkicks did 'The Gauntlet', a Clash-like exhortation of We-ain't-gonna-take-it-no-more emotions, a tune about folk who'd rather fight and die than wait too long or put up with things the way they are, the fascists snapped to attention like alsatians. Unlike the Irish muttonheads, the fascists were fighting fit and dangerously co-ordinated with one another. They put up a brief efficient fight which, in ten minutes, cleared the pit of all opposition. The fatties put up a magnificent struggle; essentially they were so weighty that shifting them against their will was a big job.

The first signs of give came when the front row of fatties collapsed over onto the stage, causing some of the equipment to topple over. They were hauled away swiftly or restored to the vertical by the band and others in the pit. As the fascists punched their way in, the fight went out of the Irish. You could tell from the looks of grim exhaustion on their sad sweaty faces that they were way too out of condition to survive the controlled muscle power that the others were flexing. Their hopeless plight, in the face of *real* tough guys in action, betrayed them for the pathetic schmucks they were.

The Dropkicks proceeded with their set surrounded by these wild guys who looked like they'd just come from robbing a bank. These were serious adults who owned vans and had wives and children, responsibilities like the Dropkicks themselves. The aspirational lyrics with their messages of triumphing over adversity, spoke strongly to them.

The pit changed character again shortly after that. Lars Fredericksen came on to do some cameo guitar with the Dropkicks so the pretty punks jumped like feisty rabbits back into the middle of the pit where they took their chances with the Nazis and the black guys who also took this opportunity to have a go. The blacks seemed to be pretty mellow individuals whose presence possibly saved the punks from a lot of shit.

As Al Barr was pointing out, it was way past midnight by this stage so we were well into St. Patrick's Day. This caused the Dropkicks to descend into various Irish ballads which drove me towards the exit. I left at the same time as two of the thin Irish with the Clancy Brothers caps. They looked like two complete idiots but turned out to be nice enough and lively enough guys.

We walked together towards the subway, worn out from the heat and the lack of oxygen. They'd been in the pit at various times I'd not bothered. One of them explained to me that heavy rock in New York was very much dependent on the various ethnic divisions in the city. A band like Pantera would have a strong Italian following, Sepultura would never have broken America so big without their core Latino following, and the Dropkick Murphys are obviously popular with Irish Americans. Also, it seems, they're popular with Puerto Ricans who regard themselves as being Irish. The odd thing about this theory, my Clancy Brothers pals said, was that many Irish also regard the Puerto Ricans as being Irish.

Doomsday Diablos –
Underground Hardcore

I had an arrangement to meet Rodrigo which came right out of *Mission Impossible.* I was to go to The Continental in the East Village for a gig by Murphy's Law, a veteran hardcore punk act I'd seen and liked twice before. Around 1 a.m. I was to meet up with Rodrigo, who would be wearing a Minor Threat T-shirt. I would be wearing my favourite I Hate You And I Hate Your Jesus T-shirt. We were to meet right under the framed poster for the gig that Iggy Pop did in The Continental in '98. Rodrigo was also, I knew, going to be a Latino, while I had a shaved head and a long black goatee. More than half the people in The Continental had a goatee and/or were Latino.

I arrived in time for The Lower East Side heroes, LES Stitches, locally popular punks endorsed by Joey Ramone and sometimes produced by Ramones/Misfits collaborator Daniel Ray. Whereas loads of the commercially successful punks – even the good ones – are carbon copies of the founding fathers (Rancid just like The Clash, Green Day and The Offspring just like The Knack, etc.), the Stitches sounded like they'd soaked up the best that punk had to offer, while keeping it all very New York and very today. The razor-thin lead singer was a nerdy combination of Richard Hell and Johnny Rotten.

About two hundred young kids gathered in the pit to

support them. Boys about 15 sang the words of all their songs as they bounced off one another in good humour. The girls made up about 45 per cent of the crowd. Taking no prisoners, they were generally tough and competitive in the pit. There was a lot of badly organised but entertaining crowd surfing which didn't coalesce until the Stitches were well into their set. The lead singer, stripped to the waist and sporting polyester purple junkie-style thrift store trousers, began to jump onto his fans about every five minutes. This had the effect of drawing the crowd closer to the stage until there was eventually an excited crush right there.

I noticed from the start that the singer was reading face after face, scanning the pit for reaction or pals. This was something he had the luxury of doing in his small venue position. He worked the pit like a whore, ranting at them a lot, rambling on about his family, introducing his sister who used to sing with them but who now lives in Florida and has just flown in for the night. He grinned maniacally every time he made to stage dive. You couldn't miss the fact that he was about to jump. The grin was like, "OK, I'm going to jump now so catch me."

When the Stitches came off they went downstairs to an open-plan basement dressing room they shared with the other bands on the five-band bill. Most of the crowd from the pit followed them into the basement where there were a few tapes and T-shirts casually on sale. The Stitches were not a major capitalist operation. Most of the action seemed to involve just talking. Girls wanting what girls want in those situations and guys wanting what they want.

By midnight the upstairs had filled up with a lot of thirtyish skinheads and younger black leather punks. I'd already checked out the famous Iggy poster which stood to the right of the stage. On the same wall there were loads of photos of other stars who've played the venue but none of them was of quite the same vintage as Mr Pop, who got pride of place. I was on the lookout for Rodrigo but there wasn't a Minor Threat T-shirt in sight. Murphy's Law took over the stage, taking a while to organise themselves. Eight tall leggy women in their late twenties lined up on the left side of the small stage but weren't getting in the way of the band. They were band wives, girlfriends, and sisters, cowering on the stage because they wanted to get a good look at the band and the floor space was about to erupt into the most brutal pit I'd ever seen.

I'd seen Murphy's Law at least twice before. They always struck me as a very violent proposition with a lightweight interface; tough, kid-friendly and able to go with the flow. As they ambled around the stage in The Continental they were just like I remembered them, blue-collar guys making music for the sake of it. Punk troubadours who travel the world preaching for a punk planet.

Between the time when the Stitches left the stage and Murphy's Law took control, there had been a notable shift within the crowd in the pit. Although a fair number of the weirdo kids still hung around, especially a little gang of cheeky rich Jewish kids who looked hard and capable, more and more of the thirtyish skinheads were moving unsubtly into the space. Not all of them were well mannered or seemed to be able to put two words together.

Normally, in the best of all possible worlds, the pit is the very essence of friendliness. If you're standing in the pit waiting for the band to come on, you only have to look at somebody and they'll start talking to you. The big boys who were infiltrating the pit at The Continental had no interest in talking. They looked at strangers, at women, at the thin kids, with bovine resentment. They were dumb mutts from dead-end jobs on dead-end street who resented whatever lives the rest of us had. Humour, sex, inferiority, money, and book reading were concepts unknown to them. If I was a woman of any kind, or even a reasonably clean altar boy, I'd hate to run into some of these characters down a back alley late at night.

Murphy's Law blasted forth like a nuclear bomb. They're a traditional New York hardcore band. Very tight with some good songs though, in general, one tune drifted into the next. They howled out their vocals concerning issues like "We ain't gonna take it no more" over flailing powerful riffs and the grindcore assault of the rhythm section. You couldn't hold their lack of originality against them – one good idea has always been enough to found a whole genre in any art form. As Bob Dylan once said, what can't be imitated perfect must die.

From the first note the pit was in a state of complete disarray. The more intellectual kids were not giving up their hard-won spaces too easily but the mammoths had methods of their own for getting you out of the way. I'd established myself in front of the stage during the break. Most of the folk doing the same thing were leftover Stitches fans, some Blacks and Latinos, and maybe thirty per cent bozos. As Murphy's Law raged on many other bozos moved forward, arms and elbows raised into a fight pose, elbowing the enemy out of the way by using sheer force of muscle and flab to move people. I got caught in a pincer movement by two enormous skinheads in their late teens who didn't so much push me out of the way as use their leverage to defeat me. Like the roller brushes in a Car Wash, they caught me in their traction, twisted me around, and spat me out. Next thing I knew I was standing behind, rather than in front of, them, and they were punching the shit out of two very thin boys, one of whom had a pink mohawk and a Sick Of It All T-shirt, who were refusing to yield.

It was quite an achievement for them to move me so effortlessly. I've loads of pit skills and I'm not exactly petite or delicate. I was glad in a way that I got shifted. A similar windmill technique used by other monsters who lurked right behind my conquerors conveyed me right into the middle of a large pit holding three hundred of the five hundred in the venue.

A powerful punch that missed my head but left a welt on my left shoulder was fair warning. The last time I'd been in a situation so confused or out of control was back in the Seventies when I participated in an actual riot following a political protest. Staying in the Murphy's Law pit involved suffering the results of the sort of one-on-one fist-fight you might have had with an aggressive individual. Only here every man in the pit – mature working guys often in prime condition – was punching or kicking at you with the idea of hitting home. This was certainly nothing like the violent posturing I'd seen in pits where people were making kicking or punching gestures that *might* catch you but where the guys were in fact indulging in a very sophisticated, risky, sort of dancing.

I was supping with tigers, not for the last time that night. You could tell from the way they approached a punch, whether they were delivering or receiving that punch, that they were comfortable with breaking jaws or crushing noses. There was a whole other male sound in the pit you could hear over the chainsaw buzz of the band's PA. This was the sound of flesh slapping against flesh, short urgent grunts of "Uh!" and "Fuck!", and the noise of punches landing in a slow remorseless staccato. It was very much the sound of sex, if you left out the punches and the lack of basic affection.

A little bit of this was plenty so I moved to the periphery of the fighting. It was almost 1 a.m. I glanced over at the Iggy poster which stood in occupied territory where the combat was total. For certain, in any case, there were no Latinos over there in Minor Threat T-shirts. The pit was now entirely white, pitbull Irish and pure Aryan. Minor Threat with their delicate ideals about lifestyle behaviour had no place in this entertaining hellhole. The punks, girls, minorities, gays, and miscellaneous others – indeed the entire agenda of progressive political causes – were consigned to the fringe.

Some of the more subterranean kids I knew from the London scene had hooked me up via e-mail with the Doomsday Diablos, a covert street gang-style posse of mainly Latino moshers. I was told about them by a black Brazilian guy, Luis, that I met in the pits at multi-band Epitaph gigs. Luis was bass player in a hardcore band, who seemed to tour a bit, that had a few indie singles out in Brazil. I reckoned from the amount of leisure time Luis could spend with me plus the endless array of cool trainers and clothes that he and his pals sported that he was a rich kid, coming from the more Beastie Boys aspect of hardcore. He was at the centre of a multiculti posse of moshers all of whom could mark your cards on scenes in different countries.

"You go to New York you'd be missing out if you didn't meet up with the Doomsday Diablos," Luis laughed. "You think you want to know about moshing then you should put in some time with those guys. If you like the thing extreme I know you'll be into their trip. I spent time hanging around with them and it was totally profound. I used to go out with this girl who was part of their scene." Luis fixed me up with all the e-mail details on them, so I'd made my date with Rodrigo weeks before.

About ten minutes after the band finished and the pit cleared I saw Rodrigo leaning against the wall right alongside Iggy. I'd been told that the Diablos were pretty intense and heavy – it was a fight club scenario. For some reason I'd expected them to be older or somehow militant. Rodrigo was a tall thin kid about 18. He'd moved to Brooklyn from Mexico when he was five. His folk were Indians from the south, so for all the world Rodrigo looks like a cross between Geronimo and Joey Ramone.

The Continental emptied out pretty quickly after Murphy's Law so we made our way to the exit. Rodrigo said he'd enjoyed the gig but thought it was all a bit traditional. "Not exactly challenging." He shrugged his shoulders against the bitter wind. "Those guys don't exactly know the meaning of fun, they're not exactly humorous, are they?"

The subway taking us across the East River was closed for repairs so we climbed up onto the great height of the Williamsburg Bridge, walking into Brooklyn on the top rung of a huge suspension bridge. I looked down from on high onto the barrios where Rodrigo and his family lived. It was about 2.30 a.m., the streetlights illuminated the deserted streets, but I could still hear loads of music drifting across the water. Mainly a kind of Hispanic hip hop in the Cypress Hill tradition.

It took us 20 minutes to cross the Bridge. As we did so we talked about the Santana High School shootings. All the rage in the media and amongst kids at gigs right then, the Santana High killings had taken place three weeks earlier, on March 5, 2000. A 15-year-old geek fired about 30 shots, killing two of his fellow pupils and wounding another 13. It was an evident Columbine High copycat. One of many that season.

Marilyn Manson had been pilloried over Columbine, amid claims that the killers were admirers of his work. This turned out to be urban myth, fabrication, and media hype. The funny thing about the Santana shootings, insofar as there was anything funny about it, was that the Santana High killer actually *did* enjoy a prominent metal act. He liked Linkin Park, one of the dippiest of all nu/rap-metal bands. They'd been called the first nu-metal boy band. I saw them supporting The Deftones, drowned out by the high-pitched screams of five thousand schoolgirls. Artistically, they were really down there in the second division, perfect MTV fodder for kids who know no better. After Santana High they were the latest band caught up in the media's obsessive interest in the disputed link between rock music and adolescent violence.

The San Diego Sheriff's Office told *Kerrang* that they only know of one band that the killer listened to, and that was Linkin Park. "One of his girlfriends made mention of it on national television," a spokesman said. "Nobody has yet said anything about the band having any kind of influence. People listen to all kinds of bands – I listen to some really weird stuff but I've never gone out and killed anybody."

Rodrigo says people were all in a tizzy because it happened in a white middle-class school.

> *"If that shit happened in the high school I went to, do you think anybody would give a fuck if the killer listened to Sepultura or Cypress Hill or shit? This has all to do with the students being white. In those schools, the white schools, you have sports as the big deal. That's why these problems in rap metal crowds happen. The women groping and the one-sided aggression. You have these sports jocks who just want to mosh for the sports aspect of it. So they don't give a fuck about punching people. They're there to do a few rounds with some poor little punk faggot, dude! Fucking assholes. So in those schools sports are everything because, through sport, the morons get on in life. People like me with working-class parents are the losers. We're filed away under 'Loser'. Then you have those other white guys who feel all inadequate and listen to shit music like Linkin Park or Marilyn Manson. They think they're so fucking weird and sensitive. When in fact they're just stupid fucking nobodies who have nothing more important to worry about other than do they fucking look cool enough, have they got the right trainers, why does everybody hate them, what cool CD should they get with their pocket money next week."*

Rodrigo had to work two jobs – an evening job and a weekend job – to get through school. In his school it was 55 per cent Latino, 20 per cent Black, 15 per cent Asian, the rest white. There was a shooting at least once a month and two students were killed during Rodrigo's time there. Another committed suicide. The issues of tragic youth and beauty which inspired the Columbine and Santana killers had no place in his world. "These fucks who go shooting up their pals because they're so fucking unhappy," Rodrigo spat out as we descended from the Bridge onto street level. "I think it's good that he was into those fucks in Linkin Park. Maybe it'll do them some damage. They are exactly the sort of band that a fuck like that would be into."

We hit the barrios west of Bedford Avenue, heading towards the East River. It was 3.15 a.m. now so the streets were emptying. A few clubs and cafes were still humming on streets full of chi-chi art galleries, pubs, and hardware stores. There was loads of music pouring out of private houses. The people on the streets were occasional Latino youths in cheap hip-hop gear, geeky art student types, and Hassidic Jewish youth marching around in groups of three or four. It was a half Latino and half impoverished bohemians part of town. After walking through ever quieter and quieter streets we reached a small park on the banks of the East River where we had a rendezvous with other members of the Doomsday Diablos.

It was mean and pinched down by the park which was located right next to a huge sugar plant, on the site of a former ferry port. There were lots of people milling around and it was well lit up. One gang of black youths gathered around a bonfire listening to pretty poor hip hop off a huge loud ghetto blaster. Some arty Sonic Youth geeks were sitting on a park bench smoking dope while using the words "totally" and "like" as if they were going out of style. A good deal closer to the river's edge about 15 guys hung out. All teenagers, they were Latino except for a Somali youth known as Little Mogadishu. They didn't have a ghetto blaster spurting out their hardcore, they didn't wear a uniform style though expensive sports gear was much in evidence, and they weren't necessarily all the best of pals. There was tension between them. The thought crossed my mind that I was the cause of the tension. Most of them had tight cropped or skinhead hair though there were some longhairs. I saw two Napalm Death and two Suicidal Tendencies T-shirts.

We quit the park pretty sharpish in two large black vans stashed around the corner. I was put in the front along with Rodrigo and the driver, a sullen white punk called Curtis who had nothing to say for himself. Slayer, Wu Tang Clan, and Trail Of Dead competed on a mixtape he slapped into the car stereo. We headed down Grand Street towards Queens and after that I was lost. Fifteen minutes later we ground to a halt outside an old warehouse building on a deserted back street full of similar warehouses.

Three slightly older long-haired guys were gathered at the entrance of the building. One of them flung open a big old wooden door to let me in. Inside was a cramped punk club with about one hundred people moshing to a DJ who was playing a savage cocktail of New York hardcore, punk, and skacore. This moshing that goes on to records in clubs is a different phenomenon from the thing that goes on in front of live bands. The main obvious difference is the lack of a crowded space around a stage. Also missing is the chemistry that goes with real human beings playing instruments they know like the back of their hands in their all-too-human way. It is because of that synergy – live music – that rock survived its dog days to thrive again today.

DJ-based moshing is very dangerous. You'd think to look at it that, with more space to play in and with the collective atmosphere of the pit missing, people would survive better. But dancing and moving so frantically without the social interplay of the pit drags people off into a zone of their own where they can do themselves specific injuries. Moshing in clubs often involves Ecstasy/Acid type drugs, and the injuries that arise are reminiscent of the ones we heard about during the great

Ecstasy-related media witch-hunts. During December 2000 a twenty-five-year-old attending the Karisma nightclub in England moshed himself to death. The club hired only DJs, never had live music, but the hospital reported that the victim died of a brain haemorrhage brought on by strenuous activity.

Rodrigo disappeared into some tense looking negotiations; there was more of a drug atmosphere about this place than arises at a lot of metal matters. I asked Little Mogadishu what the club was called and he told me it was not a club. All the people there were members of the Doomsday Diablos and their pals. They'd squatted the entire warehouse for two years. When the inevitable happened and they eventually got thrown out of this place they'd just move to another similar space. The district was full of deserted warehousing. About twice a year an inspector from the real estate firm that owned their warehouse came around and they gave him a kickback to keep his mouth shut.

Little Mogadishu lead me towards a side room where thirty guys were gathered around a flickering strobe light. In here the music was the nastiest possible sound, little more than an electronic techno staccato with growled incomprehensible vocals over the beat. Most of the guys were stripped to the waist, several were in baggy shorts. They were covered in sweat and a little blood, and they were punching the shit out of one another. It was rough but nothing like the messy nonsense we'd seen at The Continental earlier. These were dexterous early twenties guys who'd obviously trained at boxing or martial arts. Most of the time their fists and feet missed one another but when contact was made it was made in raw syncopation with the music. And it sounded really nasty. When Little Mogadishu bade me farewell and disappeared back out into the dance floor I sat down on the ground in an unlit corner where I didn't stand out too much. Maybe eight other people, mainly women, sat on the ground near me. They were rightly enthralled by the sweat and pain of a spectacle that was part *Fight Night* and part *Spartacus*.

Nobody gave an inch. The looped music grew more and more frenetic as the moshing speeded up and grew confusing. There was just no question of a girl or a young boy entering into this arena unless they'd trained well in martial arts. People were getting hurt, but not in any obviously grievous way. Also it was not squalid or gross. It was certainly elegant after a fashion. Eventually I snapped out of it and quit that chamber.

Back in the main room it was much as before. It was getting on for five when I realised that the hardcore mosh room I'd been in was one of three similar chambers. The others were still smaller rooms where well built young guys were dancing like Mohammed Ali and punching with similar power. I didn't see any teeth flying but there were occasional *Raging Bull*-style blood spurts going around. Minor Threat T-shirts or not, there was nothing straight edge about the Diablos. All this moshing and brutality was fuelled by copious amounts of spirits, speed, and grass. I didn't notice a bar anywhere or any obvious dealers. Most people brought whatever they wanted with them.

By dawn it had totally died down and there were just 30 of us sitting around on battered old couches. There were some dub reggae CDs playing through the PA and Rodrigo was giving me an assessment of the Latino metal scene in New York where a local band, Ill Nino, are doing well.

"The name of Sepultura still stands for something in Brooklyn, the Bronx, and Queens," Rodrigo laughed, with reference to the brother-against-brother feud between Soulfly and Sepultura. He had loads more besides to say about his own scene that was interesting but it was around seven so I've forgotten most of it.

Rodrigo's girlfriend Tina drove me home in one of the

black vans. Rodrigo came along for the ride, writing down the details of gigs I should go to, how to get there and what the scenario would be like. He also wrote out his mobile phone number saying, "Hey man, you know, those fucking Linkin Park are the agents of Satan, my man! Wait and see!"

Mayhem Marketing;
Limp Bizkit/Big Day Out

Limp Bizkit conquered the world and went around that world leaving a reputation for recklessness behind them. In Australia on January 26, 2000, at their Big Day Out gig a lot of their fans were injured during a set at Sydney's RAS Showgrounds. A fifteen-year-old girl suffered a heart attack during the show and subsequently died in hospital. Twelve others were taken to hospital with minor injuries after sections of the crowd twice collapsed. Among those taken to hospital were two people with fractured sternums and a ten-year-old.

Bizkit's lead vocalist Fred Durst has built up an unenviable reputation for violence and bad grace. Durst grew up surrounded by violence. His father was a drug cop and Fred served in the US Navy. He has strong memories of what it was like to see his father coming home injured: "I've seen him come home shot when I was real young, and I've seen the people he had to deal with because of drugs and stuff, and that kept me out of it. He's been shot a couple of times and he'd come home from the hospital, and you're like, 'Holy Shit'. There were crazy raids and shit. The drug dealers attacked him. It was just crazy shit."

He told *Request* magazine: "I remember the first fight I got in. I was in sixth grade and some kid got me in a headlock and I couldn't get out. He thought he had won, but I went up to him when he was at baseball practice a couple of weeks later, and I picked up a baseball bat and cracked him right in the knees."

He was a white trash adolescent dipping into various street corner societies in smalltown North Carolina. "There was a jock scene and a bad-boy redneck scene and a black scene," he recalled. "Until the Beastie Boys came out I was called 'nigger lover'. I would get ganged by so many fuckin' people. I learned how to fight good."

One critic reviewing an early support slot from Limp Bizkit commented: "The one attention-grabbing moment of Limp Bizkit's rap/thrash show was when the lead vocalist expressed a desire for gay men to be 'stomped'. Which isn't remotely rebellious. It's just puerile."

From the moment they got a record deal, the band began to draw rough crowds, albeit crowds notable for having a lot more women in them than other metal and hardcore bands. Speaking to the Spinal Column website in '97, guitarist Wes Borland (a more mellow individual than Durst with roots in Minor Threat/Metallica style music) described their European fans.

> *"You can take the biggest, nastiest, gnarliest person in the States, like a big huge punk three hundred-pound motherfucker . . . and he would just be dwarfed by the intensity of the guys over there. There were people who had these spike implants in their head. It won't be long before it's cool to cut your fingers off or something like that. It's unreal. Like little girls with scarification, branded tattoos and stuff. A little intense."*

The intensity began to cause the band problems for the first time when they joined the '98 Ozzfest along with Tool, Ozzy Osbourne, and Soulfly. At one stage Ozzy's manager and wife Sharon Osbourne considered dropping them from the tour because Ozzfest was a seated show and Bizkit fans didn't want to sit down. According to Wes Borland: "The Ozzfest has seats, and we almost got kicked off the first two days of the tour for getting the kids to break through the barricades. Sharon Osbourne was pretty angry with us because we almost incited riots."

Writing on his own website Marilyn Manson attacked the entire basis of Bizkit's bloody rise. He said: "The kind of illiterate apes that beat your ass in high school for being a 'fag' now sell you tuneless testosterone anthems of misogyny and pretend to be outsiders in a world that they were born to wear their ADIDAS-FILGERING uniforms in. And we buy it up, helplessly."

In St Paul Minnesota in July '99 Durst was accused of attacking a security guard. He allegedly kicked the guard in the head. According to the St Paul police he then told the crowd: "I kicked that punk-ass security guard in the head. That fucking bitch, you ain't gonna get a cheque tonight. Where's that fucking security guard? Where is that fucking pussy bitch?" At least one witness backed up the guard's claim that the assault was unprovoked. In April 2000 Durst and the injured guard – who received treatment in hospital for blurred vision and equilibrium difficulties – reached an out of court settlement.

Wes Borland commented of Durst's temper and violent streak: "Fred will sometimes totally explode and try to knock the monitor guys over the head with a microphone stand, or he'll attack people onstage. Sometimes he'll walk off after just one song or he'll break every microphone at a huge show on purpose and just not sing."

June '99 Limp Bizkit undertook a "guerrilla style" tour of America, which involved, in any given city, announcing a surprise rooftop gig on the local radio an hour before the band started playing. According to a press release from their label Interscope after one of these shows there were: "3,000 to 5,000 screaming fans before the cops shut them down. At approx. 4 p.m. radio station WAAF announced the location, and kids began pouring in from all directions, blocking streets, sidewalks, store and restaurant entrances – even climbing lampposts to get better views. At approx. 5 p.m. the gig began, continuing for about 25 minutes, though fans were still converging on the scene from all directions even after police pulled the plug . . ."

The strategy behind this tour, to "play until you get shut down", was based around the U2 video for 'Where The Streets Have No Name', wherein U2 played that number on an LA urban rooftop until the cops shut them down, which made a big impression on Fred Durst. The other cultural reference (as with U2) was to The Beatles' iconic final live performance, filmed for their movie *Get Back,* played live on the roof of their Apple headquarters in London in 1969.

Durst developed a reputation for encouraging audiences to lose control. On the '99 Family Values tour he told the audience: "I can tell you motherfuckers are out of control and that's what I like to see." Another time he told the crowd to "show the whole world how much we can fuck up a baseball field."

In the months following their notorious set at Woodstock '99 a lot of people began to suggest that Limp Bizkit were a band in search of a disaster. Kurt Loder of MTV said of their behaviour: "I thought the Limp Bizkit performance was pushing a lot of cheap buttons and was the most reprehensible thing I had seen." Durst told the Woodstock crowd: "Don't let anybody get hurt. But I don't think you should mellow out. That's what Alanis Morissette had you motherfuckers do. If someone falls pick 'em up. We already let the negative energy out. Now we wanna let out the positive energy."

Drummer John Otto is on record as saying that the Woodstock riots were totally cool. In *Drum!* magazine he said: "We started a song and then stopped because Fred was going, 'Hey, can you all hear me?' And nobody could. Well people started to get pissed. Then they turned it back on. Just total chaos broke out, MTV people were running for their lives, *Much Music* people were running for their lives . . . It was totally cool."

In a classic example of mayhem management, Bizkit's next video – *Re-arranged* – was a cheeky response to the umbrage they endured after Woodstock. *Re-arranged* features each member of the band in a separate prison cell awaiting sentence for their part in the riots. Adopting the role of beleaguered outsider artist – rather than rich reactionary Vice President of Interscope Records – Durst said the video was "about being persecuted for something you're not guilty of. No matter how hard anybody tries to get rid of Limp Bizkit, which everyone is trying to do, we're gonna live forever."

Gary Bongiovanni, editor of the touring industry magazine *Pollstar*, a somewhat controversial commentator on the live scene, hit the nail on the head when he said about post-Woodstock Limp Bizkit: "No promoter would refuse to promote a Limp Bizkit date at this point in time. The band's hot and they're selling tickets. The danger is if they develop a reputation where they might be considered a threat to public safety, and that really hasn't happened. People forgive an isolated incident. If it becomes a pattern, then people get concerned."

It was about to become a pattern.

Big Day Out is a Lollapalooza-style touring festival which, each summer, moves between Australia's major cities. Suggestions that the kids who go to Big Day Out are in some way reckless or ferocious have no real foundation in fact. After Big Day Out '99 a Christian posted *Where Was God at the Big Day Out?* to www.salvos.com, the Salvation Army's website. This said that Big Day Out '99 was marked by the same kind of crowd chaos that subsequently caused death and injury, but also gave evidence of the solidarity which makes moshing a good and sociable thing: "It was quite moving to see people wrenched from the floor by their T-shirts after crowd-surfing, with the words, 'Are you right, mate?' It was equally moving to have people say, 'Excuse me, please', as they surged forward towards the stage." According to this report not only was there real "crowd etiquette" amongst these moshers who were looking after one another, but there was also a genuine affection for other people not getting involved in the pit. Then again, a Christian might say that.

At Big Day Out '99 the headliners, Red Hot Chili Peppers, stalled their set until the crowd moved backwards to prevent crushes at the front. It wasn't until this had been achieved that Anthony Kiedis led the band into their great anthems such as 'Scar Tissue' and 'Under The Bridge'.

On the same day that Limp Bizkit saw a girl die during their set, on one of the Big Day Out side stages, media darlings At The Drive-In indulged in their usual middle-class anti-moshing rhetoric. Their guitarist Jim Ward expressed his doubts about the remorseless presence of the mosh pit and all that it entails: "It gets frustrating having to fight it all the time, and if it gets to the point where it's taking from us wanting to be onstage then we're going to have to stop touring. And our next album will be a reaction to this, it won't be as hard, I can guarantee it." At The Drive-In began their set by telling the crowd: "Take care of each other and don't beat the shit out of each other." During a club date on the same trek through Australia, At The Drive-In asked moshers to leave the gig and offered them refunds.

When the creative energy and musical violence of At The Drive-In was reflected by the Big Day Out crowd in terms of moshing, the band turned ratty and vocalist Cedric Bixler attacked, first the photographers, and then the audience whom he started making baa-ing sounds at. At The Drive-In quit the stage after a few songs, the audience erupting into boos and roars of "Bullshit".

Before Limp Bizkit played the crowd in the pit was swirling around in a lethal cocktail of too much heat, heavy drinking, and a generally dark atmosphere of excitement and anticipation. All hell broke loose when the band actually walked out onto the stage.

A photographer working in the security pit between the crowd barriers and the front of stage said: "Limp Bizkit were into their first song. This crush began in a concentrated area at the front of the stage in a five metre area along the barrier fence. Girls were falling over and big blokes with tattoos were falling over them. It was getting frightening. I heard a stage manager talking on a headset asking, 'Tell me, mate, what's going on, what's going on?' Then he yelled out, 'Stop the band, stop the band, stop them now, there's people going down.'"

"You guys gotta help each other out because the security here sucks. Fuck these security guards, we can take care of ourselves," said Durst.

"Hold up guys, we just gotta work out a problem," said Durst when the band were two songs into their set. "If you see somebody fall down you gotta make sure you pick them up." An unidentified disembodied voice from the PA said: "Everybody just be patient. Things are getting out of hand . . . step back a few steps, people are down in front."

Five minutes later the band were given the all-clear to start again but, rather than calming down, the crowd seemed to rise up to a new level of rage as the band moved into their hugely controversial 'Break Stuff'. The song climaxed with the crowd screaming to the band: "Give me something to break!" Two thirds of the 55,000 plus throng erupted into moshing. This was really dangerous. After 'My Generation', Durst was forced one more time to talk with his crowd: "Stop again guys. Once again we're having a bit of trouble at the front."

This time the band took a ten-minute break, causing hollers of "Bullshit", and booing from the crowd. Although injured people were being dragged out of the pit in front of his very eyes, Durst's comment on regaining the stage was a spiteful, "About fucking time."

The Big Day Out organisers claimed that: "The performance was of sufficient intensity to provoke unprecedented and ferocious crowd activity in front of the stage." This was a major compliment of sorts. It gives the impression that Limp Bizkit are one of those transcendent acts who deliver dementia-inducing live performances. In fact they are a very plastic and derivative combination of Kid Rock and The Beastie Boys without the creativity of one or the humour of the other. Ill-educated white trash kids are inclined to say that Limp Bizkit speak for them, *are* them. There is something lumpen and vulgar about the band's onstage assault on the audience.

In the Sydney mosh pit kids were fighting for their lives but the festival security seemed to regain control. Just after 9 p.m. security guards pulled Jessica Michalik from the seething pit. She was carried into the St John Ambulance area by the stage, where it was found that she had no pulse. They pumped oxygen into her lungs and brought her back to life with an adrenaline injection. Fred Durst told the crowd to "chill out" as Michalik was being treated.

A witness said: 'It was like a war scene in the tent. There were 25 kids on their backs. Drips were being connected to them. It looked like a mass resuscitation was going on. It was absolute pandemonium."

Kirsten Hambridge, who believed that she was caught up in the crowd crush which killed Jessica Michalik, wrote an article about her experience for Sydney's *Sun Herald*: "I was howling with pain. I couldn't breathe. Then I heard someone behind me say this could be another Pearl Jam. I thought, I gotta get out of here. My friend was lifted out. But people were falling over me and pinning me down." Hambridge was screaming at a security guard to get her out: "He couldn't get me out and started to walk away. I screamed, 'Get me out of here or I'm going to die.' I freed one arm and grabbed him by the shirt, and pulled him over."

Jessica Michalik's father told ABC that his daughter didn't like mosh pits. Mr Michalik believed that Jessica was drawn into the mosh pit and overwhelmed by the chaos. This kind of thing *does* happen accidentally all the time at big gigs. Then again, mosh pits contain within themselves such huge energy and vitality that people can be drawn, despite their more sensible instincts, right into the middle of real tight situations. Crowds like that are inevitably full of people who've taken loads of drugs or too much booze.

Limp Bizkit quit the Big Day Out tour, which still had three days to run, before the death of Jessica Michalik was announced. They said they'd spoken to the Big Day Out promoters about crowd safety a week earlier. They'd requested additional security personnel and a t-shaped security barrier which would have allowed security staff to operate in a catwalk-style space extending down into the middle of the arena.

In a self-defensive statement they said: "After careful consideration and numerous demands to Big Day Out promoters to bolster security measures, Limp Bizkit have decided not to perform the remaining three days of the festival. Shaken by the injuries that occurred and what the band perceived as a cavalier attitude toward fan safety by festival organisers, Limp Bizkit ultimately do not have confidence that the last three days of the six-day event will run smoothly with no one harmed."

Durst said he had "begged" for safety measures to be increased but was told that the promoters had been doing the event for ten years and that they knew what they were doing. He said: "Though we tried to explain that crowds are different from ten – or even three – years ago, we were ultimately frustrated by his response. Any promoter who sticks his head in the ground and refuses to believe that audiences have changed is asking for tragedy."

It is unlike Durst to make a legitimate point in the midst of his all-too-familiar defence of Limp Bizkit's outrageous crowd-baiting and subsequent mayhem marketing. But it is very true that hardcore audiences, and what happens in the pit, changes radically all the time. The music, and the reaction of the pit to that music, is changing fast, just like hip hop and its related violence escalated hand-in-hand during the golden age of that genre. Middle-aged festival promoters all over the world have already paid a heavy price for their arrogant notion that they know what time it is. Quite simply, a festival today featuring Limp Bizkit, Korn, or The Deftones bears scant resemblance to one five years back which might have had the likes of the Chili Peppers, Beastie Boys, or Metallica. In the aftermath a Big Day Out co-promoter, Vivian Lees, the very man who told Bizkit he knew what he was doing, seemed to agree that he was out of touch with new trends.

"The behaviour of the crowds at these events is becoming more radical," he said. "It's becoming very serious and, as a father myself, this is a huge distress to me."

While Durst put up his verbal defensive barricades, family and friends gathered in a garden near Sydney's Concord Hospital where Michalik lay on a life support system. A family friend said: "We are hoping for a miracle."

Big Day Out founder and organiser Ken West said that Bizkit's proposed use of a T-shaped barrier designed to split the audience in two was untested and untried in Australia: "It would have been heartbreaking for us to go against what we know. We can't just try out something that someone says they want, and risk ending up with a worse situation." It was rightly pointed out that, "The measures proposed by Limp Bizkit were substantial, untested and radical changes to the existing structures and procedures in place for the show as understood by the Australian safety authorities."

Big Day Out initially commended Limp Bizkit for their "full cooperation . . . through this difficult situation and their commitment to the safety of their audience," but in a later statement the organisers expressed "relief at the departure of Limp Bizkit."

After hearing about Michalik's death Fred Durst spoke with her parents and the band issued another statement: "We are devastated that Jessica died . . . The loss of her life will impact ours forever."

On the Limp Bizkit website he posted another clarification: "We pulled out because a girl died at our show because of shitty security. We told the Big Day Out security to make it better and they said to piss off."

Durst went on the US TV show, *Access Hollywood*, a month after the Michalik death. He said that Limp Bizkit had been victimised by Big Day Out and local cops. He said that the band did their set on the insistence of local police, who were afraid that there'd be a riot if they pulled out: "As soon as we started playing the second song we stopped. We stopped for five minutes. We saw people falling down in the front. "

He then went on to discuss, in a rather crude way, the private aspects of the tragedy for Michalik's family: "Her parents had the option to pull the plug. Because she never came to and there was serious damage, so they did."

He said that the Michalik family "are really supportive of us", and then he said that Jessica's parents "are really happy that their daughter was with her friends and seeing her favourite band when she died."

During April '01 it emerged that At The Drive-In were

taking a permanent vacation from one another. A statement talked of them going on an "indefinite hiatus". The pressures of success had got to them. Remorseless touring and internal conflicts about mellowing their sound were rumoured to have caused the split. Most people agreed that a determining factor was the depression which descended on the band after the Big Day Out tragedy. They were deeply affected by it, cancelled extensive tours shortly afterwards, and called it a day.

One month after Jessica's death Limp Bizkit and their label Interscope launched a new Internet moshing game for Bizkit fans. The winner in *Mosh Master* was the one with the least dead bodies when the game was over. One of the main rules of the game was to ignore the rules: "Avoid the security goons and get on stage, then dive into the crowd to score. If you hit the floor, you lose one life."

Deftones, March 2001

After the Big Day Out death bands in the spotlight began to feel beleaguered by moshing. They had to be so careful after that, because the stigma had definitely stuck to Pearl Jam and Limp Bizkit.

Soon upwardly mobile hardcore band's reputations, plus their ability to play the kind of extreme music they want to play, will be compromised by what is happening in the pit. Those bands are trapped by a lethal combination of their own venue-stuffing abilities and the fact that, no matter what they say about moshing from the stage, it goes on and it seems to be getting more dangerous all the time.

The Deftones have always been known as a mosh-friendly band. They were playing the biggest headline gig of their lives when I caught them on the Back To School tour. Support act was the on-the-up but otherwise irrelevant Linkin Park.

The only problem Deftones front man Chino Moreno had about diving into mosh pits was that people keep stealing the clothes off his back. At a gig in Spain they stole his belt and he had trouble keeping his trousers up. "I would never go into a crowd and steal people's shit," he said. "I understand if they want something of mine as a memento but, shit, I want Elizabeth Hurley's bra but I would never dream of stealing it from her."

Linkin Park had plenty of reasons to be worried about the

crowd surfing and heavy crowd surges which marred their set. Right then the American media was hot on their trail with a story linking their name to the latest Columbine High copycat killer. Since they were more Backstreet Boys than Chili Peppers, this was not good news for them. They played a set that went down really big with the young girls in the crowd so there was much high-pitched screeching. A longhair alongside me called them "unendurably bad". During their set four people were taken from the pit on stretchers. A girl I met told me that she was down the front and that when they took her best friend out of the pit they put a neck brace on her, that her entire body was shaking with involuntary jerking movements as they hauled her away. She also said that there were loads of people collapsing in on top of one another all around her, that it was totally frightening.

Twenty minutes into The Deftones' set the band stopped playing so that Chino Moreno could sort out things in the pit. In terms of crowd problems, they had a difficult job to do. Musically, they'd a responsibility not to play a raucous set that would kick out all the jams and let rip. They played a lot of slowish stuff and the mad punk/hip-hop fury that characterised their earlier shows was no longer in evidence. In front of such a large crowd, their normally enraged onslaught might have been too much.

Four songs later Moreno ground everything to a halt one more time, saying that people were getting into bad trouble out there in the crowd. He then pointed at a specific small group in the pit and told them what to do: "Hey you! You with the red T-shirt. Yeah you! There is a guy with long black hair right behind you, and he needs your help. Turn around, just turn right around and then you'll see him. Everybody else around him help him out."

Later Moreno stopped the show all over again. This time he got them to turn up the house lights and walked to the edge of the pit where he spent an eternity disentangling kids from one another. Some of those kids were a good half-mile away from him but he was clearly able to see what was happening to his crowd. Then he suggested that they should all quit crowd surfing: "Man, crowd surfing is old shit. People have been doing that for years. When I see film of that Pearl Jam thing, I don't want that kind of shit happening at our shows so let's forget about crowd surfing. I don't want to see that shit anymore. Think of something new to do. It's stupid and dangerous."

The following week a sixteen-year-old girl wrote a letter to *Kerrang*: "As this was one of my first gigs I didn't know what to expect, so I decided to go near to the front . . . I was taken by surprise at the ferocity of the mosh pit and after 15 minutes of struggling to stay upright I fell over. I had about five people landing on me. I was fucking scared to say the least. It was a relief then to know that some people in the crowd cared."

She went on to thank a boy who rescued her and helped her out of the pit, and to thank Moreno for sorting out all the pit problems.

This kind of high drama, this life and death struggle, is becoming a regular feature of big rock gigs all over the world. Other, more gentle, high dramas happen in mosh pits every night of the week. Moshers will no doubt, in the end, fundamentally alter the music at whose altar they worship.

Drawing Conclusions On The Wall

Why is moshing so attractive? For just one moment, after one last gulp of oxygen, when you walk out into the moshpit, you're the master of the universe. That is why moshing is so attractive.

Some years ago in Dublin I was talking rock music with two guys who'd been players in the emergent hard rock scene of the Seventies. One worked as a publicist for Led Zeppelin, Thin Lizzy and T.Rex. The other was once the drummer in a rock band that'd scored five chart albums in the US and toured with The Kinks, Blue Oyster Cult, and the J. Geils Band. Forgotten heroes of forgotten wars. But when those guys did their rock thing back in the old days, rock and what went with it was a lot of fun. Between sex and drugs the two of them had consumed an adult portion. This was not to say that the two men in question were anything other than hip and sophisticated. The drummer had come to rock out of the poetry-with-bongos scene which centred around the Liverpool and Beat poets. The publicist, a genuine-article libertine, was the brother of Ireland's leading poetry publisher.

The two guys both came from the same small Irish town where they'd grown up together in the early Sixties. They were talking about that town and about first listening as kids to Elvis and Chuck Berry on the radio. It was late at night, a lot of dope had been smoked. They both agreed that experiencing primitive rock'n'roll had changed their lives forever. A guy from a then-hip local Dublin band who was in the room challenged this, suggesting that in reality Elvis didn't change folk's lives any more than Bing Crosby had in his day.

I remember being surprised by the emotional responses this elicited from my two pals, both of whom were cynical enough veterans. They said that, but for rock'n'roll, neither would have left their small home town and made those big adventurous trips to far-flung spots like Dublin and London. They both insisted they'd have become ambition-less nobodies but for the way rock music had stirred their souls. They agreed that, because of the music, they'd seen and done incredible things. What surprised me about this outburst was the fact that these two remarkably well known and respected individuals in the rock milieu at that time retained an internalised lack of self-worth. But for the art form which swept over their entire generation, they were saying, they would have amounted to nothing. Their belief was that rock music had alchemical qualities, that it could turn dull provincials destined for suburban jobs and suburban salaries into temporary masters of the universe. The same idea, shrunk down just like rock itself has shrunk down, thrives and festers in the mosh pit today.

It is a notion which has ruined the lives of many a musician and many a fan over the last 50 years. It radiates out from the core of the art form, the actual artists who make the music. Great musicians always sit uncomfortably within the society which pays their bills. Musicians tend to be innocent outsiders capable of intense self-delusion and grand visions. The frustrations such emotions give rise to causes them to mouth off in every direction, creating an ever-mounting pile of ideas, rhetoric, bullshit, misinformation, and positive energies that their fans absorb. This absorption can alter the lives of those affected.

In times gone by the social consequences of rock have occasionally been devastating. The Sixties counterculture owed

227

everything to the notions being spouted, in the first place, by a small core of influential rock stars. In our own time rock became a demeaned currency. On the one hand we had the spectacle of pomp rock undergoing a bizarre revival as a back-drop to rabble-rousing rallies by the likes of Boris Yeltsin and Slobodan Milosovich. On the other hand an ageing elite at rock music's pinnacle refused to bow out gracefully. The form itself began to look middle-aged and slack. For the first time in 50 years a substantial minority of the smart kids out there didn't really like rock anymore.

These, not too long ago, looked like fatal symptoms. And that was where moshing came in.

What happened from the early Nineties on was that rock music, seriously under pressure from the vast explosion of artistically valid hip hop and culturally subversive techno, regrouped. It regrouped, like a guerrilla army in the hills, about the bonfires of the mosh pit. In the early days it was small crowds of fanatical followers. A lean mean rewritten music emerged which combined the taut musculature of punk with the equally tight mentality of hip hop. The elitism which had characterised rock since its beginnings was ditched in favour of a more democratic spirit. The new bands who came up from the street really did want to keep in touch with that street. Moshing was part of the means by which they kept in contact. An independent band sector thrived while the corporations signed up every compliant indie weirdo (Beck, Sonic Youth, Butthole Surfers) they could lay their hands on. This entire new scene was often driven by and for the pit.

The expectations from music were no longer as highly strung as they had been. Now it was up to you to change your own life if you wanted to. Nothing you ever heard on a record was going to achieve that for you. You started that process by becoming an activist amongst your peers in the pit.

Mosh pits from the very beginning rejected rock's elitism

and iconography. Within literal spitting distance of bands, pits could turn nasty on bands at small shows. The story of moshing is full of the vilification of superstars, and contempt for their work. It is full of that intense discussion of music and albums amongst fans which is vital to any true innovation. Moshing became an extraordinarily good influence on the quality of music being made. It would be fair to say that American rock music, in all its forms, has undergone an unexpected renaissance since the days when enthusiastic applause was all that was needed from gig attendees.

The rising popularity of moshing and the bands that go with it has raised two issues relevant to every part of society. One has to do with women. There is a new feminist sexuality rising up amongst smart young girls which rejects the platitudes of conventional society and challenges the outmoded arguments of radical feminism. You can see this tough sexuality in action at shows when girls giggle and curse in reaction to the sexual anonymity of the crowd. Rape and harassment – whole other matters – at gigs challenge society to take a long hard look at itself, not at moshing and young people.

The other issue is violence. There is a radically increased admiration of disorder at the core of mainstream white youth culture. This admiration, perhaps, has always been there. The opportunities for putting theory into practice have never been so available. Rather tedious dullards have come into the pit searching for thrills that aren't really to be had there. Should moshing be barred because it's too dangerous? No. Should it be regulated and made safe? Maybe, in the best of all possible worlds, it should be. But making moshing safe would be like picking up mercury with a fork. In any case, most efforts to make moshing safe have more to do with suppressing it rather than improving it. As Lou Reed once said: "The music is all. People should die for it. People are dying for everything else, so why not for music?"

For someone like me, who became passionately interested in music at the time of the original punk explosion, music has always been a vehicle for change. By the early Nineties I was one of many who transferred my loyalties to hip hop, having a great deal more in common with its attitude and swagger than I had with the pathetic leftovers of rock's once-mighty empire. I was as shocked as everybody else when various fringe American rock'n'roll iconoclasts reclaimed the streets and the charts.

Like my pals back in Dublin I've always reckoned that rock music acted as a catalyst taking me to nasty places where I wanted to go. There has always been an adolescent aspect to pursuing this music. I've seen prosperous and portly men in their fifties get hot under the collar about whether The Small Faces or The Who were the better band. Hip hop substantially altered my life for the good and I was convinced that rock would never again exert the same hold over me. Rock, however, is a resilient old beast and the minute I discovered moshing I was back in the thick of it all over again. I discovered a whole new world of people like myself who saw in music an excellent excuse to avoid the dull inevitability that life throws up in our faces.

In the pit I experienced a passionate and romantic commitment to a musical genre which was reminiscent, more than anything else, of the original Mod scene. As with Mod, there was a narcissism which bordered on the sexual and a tinge of violence which made it all seem that little bit dubious. I enjoyed this very much and was in my element. What did I discover in there that I didn't already know?

I discovered that, unlike the other waves of kids who got into similar scenes in the past, moshers had a very bleak vision of the future. These people thought that life was brief, boring, and pointless. The pit was real and certain magic which lasted maybe two hours. Many of them tended to come from single parent homes or homes where there was one step-parent, often the father. They came from all classes, but many of them were working-class or lower-middle-class kids who found, in the classlessness of the pit, a unique opportunity for social mobility. Most of the moshers were inevitably guys and many of these enjoyed poor relationships with their fathers. They had a very low opinion of traditional notions of masculinity, and a lot of them thought women were strange creatures. Many had such peripheral notions about how society actually worked that I genuinely worried about what would become of them. They knew a hell of a lot about good music – they educated me a lot – but their interest in stuff recorded before '90 was nonexistent.

While moshing has many strong communal aspects to it, I would agree with every mosher worth his or her salt that the thing you learn the most about in the pit is yourself. This is the real power of the pit. It is the real deal; it gives rise to a level of self-analysis long absent from rock's bag of tricks. The first time I walked into the pit I thought I was the great guy, Mr Invincible. About ten minutes later I'd been chewed up and spat out. That told me something about myself. The next time I was better prepared. I'd worked out for a while, I was wearing the right attitude, and the band was Sepultura.

Since that night I've deconstructed and reconstructed myself as a result of moshing. It cleared out both my body and soul. I got a new bounce in my step from the immense anonymous amusement I participated in. You tend to feel very much alone in the pit, a temporary autonomous zone, and you get relaxed with that lonely-in-the-crowd emotion. This is great training for the anonymous city landscape which rock music reflects. I think you don't make all that many good friends in the pit because, contrary to all the yap about brotherhood and solidarity, it is a loner pursuit. When a gang of guys heads into the pit together, they'll generally split up and meet each other outside later.

The mosh pit is certainly the latest manifestation of human-ity's desire to press the pause button on ageing. Moshing is a placebo for the life that none of us can ever have – the life that goes on forever. Neal Busch from Trail Of Dead said that the pit symbolised kids keeping themselves safe inside their own universe, aware that they were being pressurised by an outside world which wanted them to grow up, something they didn't ever want to do. I think this is very close to the mark. Since the days when people tore up cinema seats at Bill Haley concerts rock'n'roll has been the preserve of those aged between 14 and 30, all of them howling to the world about how unfair it was that they, like everybody else, must mature. The trashing of venue property, the defiance of venue security, the risking of life and limb, are potent manifestations of the indifference kids feel towards the sensible values of their seniors.

Kids I meet in the pit make regular reference to the fear that they'll have to stop moshing when they get older. I can talk to them about anything other than their jobs or school and college courses. They hear enough about that shit at home and the rest of the week. Moshing, for most of them, is a celebration of the moment, of the sad fact that it *is* only a moment. No matter how weird, special, freaky, talented or gifted with physical skills we all seem to be in the pit, we all know that someday this will be over for us. It will keep going for others, but we'll have no place there. The lights will go up and we'll just be regular guys on the street again.

When the day comes that you can no longer cut it in the pit, it will spit you out and forget about you. But for two hours in the darkness you are certainly the person you always imagined yourself to be.

Acknowledgements

I spoke and corresponded with a number of people during my travels: Neil Busch from And They Will Know Us By Our Trail Of Dead, Esquivel 666, Max Cavalera from Soulfly, Frank Rynne from Finger/Islamic Diggers, Joey Jordison from Slipknot, Brian Barry from One Minute Silence, Andreas Kisser from Sepultura, Myron/ Matt Rea from Workhorse Movement/The Dirty Americans, Ishay Berger from Useless ID, James Lister, Ill Nino.

I gave a lecture to the *Living In A Material World* conference at Coventry School of Art which partially suggested this book to me. Peter Playdon and Andrew Beck gave me that opportunity. I wrote most of *Inside The Mosh Pit* at the Chelsea Hotel in New York during March 2001. Stanley Bard and his staff provided the perfect environment. Brendan Maher at South Tipperary Arts Centre gave me technical back-up. Jason White put me on an inordinate number of guest lists. I'm very grateful to Helen Donlon, Peter Maybury, Ira Cohen, Ricardo, Darius, Daniel Figgis, Olga Buckley, Marek Pytel, Michael Murphy, Fiona Collett, Tavis Henry, Mindee Hutchinson, Jacopo Pandolfo, John Goulding, Neil McCarthy, Bill Murphey at Axiom, Regina Weinreich, Mark Burman, Stanley Booth, Matt Willis, Andrea and Sabine at IBD, Lorcan Collins, Kevin Brew, Elaine Palmer, Jamie at Roadrunner New York, all the people at the Ljubljana Kinotech, Carl Stickley, Lydia Lunch, Chamber of Pop Culture, Gary and Jizza, the Doomsday Diablos, Gene Gregorits, Paranoid Visions, Goofy Sufi, Herbert Huncke, Hamri, Markus Ohrlich at Bench Press, Karl Sinfield/EM, and Joel Pereira.

I was putting the finishing touches to this book on Easter Sunday 2001 when Joey Ramone died. When I first heard The Ramones on the radio and bought their singles they changed my feeling for music and altered my ideas about life. As recent history has shown, I was not alone in this. Joey and his brothers stood for everything this book is about. Adios amigo.

JOE AMBROSE
joedigger@hotmail.com

Sources

www.altcult.com A reliable guide to alternative culture. I relied on it.

www.crowdsafe.com The website of Crowd Management Strategies, a Chicago-based organisation lead by Paul Wertheimer. I'm uneasy about their anti-band and anti-moshing stances but I found a lot of information on Roskilde and arena/festival problems.

www.grandroyal.com Mary Chen wrote *Mosh; A Pointless Etymology*.

www.furious.com Jason Gross interviewed Ron Ashton.

www.moshersaregay.com A humorous comic-book look at moshing.

Rolling Stone did an excellent investigation of Roskilde which explained what happened there.

Kerrang provided a lot of information about One Minute Silence.

There is no discography since recorded music is a separate discipline from live performance. Most albums produced by Ross Robinson and Rick Rubin capture the thrill of live music. Some early *Flipside* videos have graphic footage of moshing at its raw best. *MAXIMUM ROCK'N'ROLL* still reports from the front line of the punk underground.